THE TWO-STEP LOW-FODMAP DIET AND RECIPE BOOK

THE TWO-STEP LOW-FODMAP DIET AND RECIPE BOOK

DR SUE SHEPHERD

CONTENTS

PART 2: TWO-STEP LOW-FODMAP RECIPES

PART 3: USEFUL INFORMATION

INTRODUCTION

The Low-FODMAP Diet is a simple treatment for irritable bowel syndrome (IBS), a condition that affects one in seven people worldwide. If you're reading this, you may already have been formally diagnosed with the condition, or you may suspect you have it (in which case, you should see your doctor for investigations and diagnosis). The classic symptoms of IBS are abdominal pain, bloating, distension, excess wind and altered bowel habits (constipation or diarrhoea or a combination of both). Sufferers of fructose, lactose and wheat intolerances may also experience similar symptoms. These days, these various conditions are seen as closely related, and the Low-FODMAP Diet is effective in treating the symptoms of all of them (except coeliac disease, see page 8).

The diet, fully explained on page 12, works on identifying then eliminating or restricting certain kinds of food that cause bowel symptoms. In the last decade, the Low-FODMAP Diet has come to be regarded, both in Australia and internationally, as the most effective dietary treatment for the symptoms of IBS, providing relief in 75 per cent of patients.

... the Low-FODMAP Diet has come to be regarded, both in Australia and internationally, as the most effective dietary treatment for the symptoms of IBS, providing relief in 75 per cent of patients.

In 2011 I wrote *Food Intolerance Management Plan*, which outlined the principles of the diet for a general audience. Since then, the term 'low-FODMAP' has become well known in the medical community and among IBS sufferers. This book is a step on from the last, offering an additional 80 brand-new low-FODMAP recipes, updates on developments, and advice on how to phase in certain kinds of foods safely in order to make the diet as accessible and sustainable as possible.

Although it may have a technical-sounding name, the Low-FODMAP Diet owes much of its success to its simplicity. It has clear rules that are easy to follow; all ingredients can be purchased in the supermarket; and the recipes are straightforward and suitable for the whole family. In this book I've included meal plans, advice for eating out and travelling, and lists of restricted and non-restricted foods.

TWO-STEP PLAN

For many, a FODMAP-modified diet will be a diet for life. After years of working as a practising dietitian and teaching the Low-FODMAP Diet, I know from experience that people are more likely to stick to diets that have fewer restrictions. The idea of the two-step approach outlined in this book is to show you how to reintroduce certain restricted ingredients into your diet gradually.

The two-step eating plan and all recipes are designed to support the individualised reintroduction of FODMAP-containing foods, as tolerated, so the diet is not restricted unnecessarily.

PART 1: ABOUT THE TWO-STEP LOW-FODMAP DIET

“I had never heard of FODMAPS until my doctor gave me a scrap of paper with the term written down and told me to go home and look it up. It has only been a month, but you have changed my life. I am no longer living with pain and inflammation on a daily basis.

The Low-FODMAP Diet has made the most incredible difference to my life. My physiotherapist is amazed at the change in me. She got all the details from me, as she said she has many patients who could benefit from a low-FODMAP lifestyle. Yesterday, I did not take a single painkiller. Thank you so much for allowing me to take my life back.”

1. FODMAPS, IBS AND THE LOW-FODMAP DIET

WHAT IS IRRITABLE BOWEL SYNDROME (IBS)?

Around one in seven Australians suffers from IBS, a broad term used to describe a cluster of persistent digestive symptoms, usually after more serious causes, such as coeliac disease (see page 8), have been eliminated. Why some people experience the often-debilitating effects of IBS is not understood, but there is now strong evidence that FODMAPs often trigger symptoms. These symptoms vary from person to person in frequency and severity. Symptoms triggered by FODMAPs usually come on at least 30 minutes after the food in question is eaten, as it takes time for the unabsorbed FODMAPs to reach the large bowel, where most of the symptoms are generated. Some FODMAPs (fructose, lactose and polyols) are poorly absorbed in some of us, while other FODMAPs (fructans and GOS) are not absorbed in *any* of us.

Why don't we all have IBS?

One of the key factors involved in the perception of symptoms is something called the 'gut–brain axis', a communication pathway between the nerves that surround the bowel and the brain. The large bowel is 'designed' to blow up like a balloon when gas is produced by the bacterial fermentation of fibre, FODMAPs, and so on. It's normal and expected that the bacteria will produce gas. The body usually deals with this gas either via the back passage (with a 'fart', 'flatus' or 'wind') or it crosses the intestine wall and dissolves in the bloodstream, then is carried up to the lungs and breathed out. Gas production is normal, and bowels blowing up and down like an inflating and deflating balloon is also normal.

Around one in seven Australians suffers from IBS, a broad term used to describe a cluster of persistent digestive symptoms, usually after more serious causes, such as coeliac disease, have been eliminated.

In some people, such as those with IBS, however, the nerves within the stretch receptors surrounding the bowel don't like the bowel blowing up like a balloon. These nerves have what's called 'visceral hypersensitivity', which means they're extra sensitive to stimuli that should really be considered normal. These ultrasensitive nerves send distress messages to the brain when the bowel is distended. The brain can do one of two things in response: recognise that these messages should be ignored, or over-interpret them and process them to generate symptoms (such as what happens in people with IBS). This nerve communication is the gut–brain axis, and in people with IBS the unhappy brain and gut can trigger IBS symptoms. In people without IBS, the gut–brain axis is functioning normally, there's no visceral hypersensitivity, and the brain doesn't over-interpret the messages, so symptoms aren't usually triggered.

Other players are also involved in IBS, and may include abnormal types and/or amounts of bacteria in the large bowel and increased permeability of the lining of the bowels and an altered immune response. How the visceral hypersensitivity begins, and the gut–brain axis becomes altered, is not well understood – many people first experience symptoms after a bad bout of gastroenteritis, some after travelling overseas, some after a long or strong course of antibiotics, and some after a physical or emotional trauma. For others, however, there's no obvious reason why their IBS started. Fortunately, the Low-FODMAP Diet is effective in resolving IBS symptoms in the majority of people who try it, regardless of the underlying cause.

Scientific studies have shown that apart from IBS symptoms, FODMAPs also trigger fatigue, lethargy and reduced concentration. Why this occurs is not well understood, however the good news is a Low-FODMAP Diet has been shown to improve these symptoms in the many people with IBS who also suffer from fatigue and 'brain fog'.

Fortunately, the Low-FODMAP Diet is effective in resolving IBS symptoms in the majority of people who try it.

DO YOU HAVE IBS?

There are many conditions that have symptoms similar to IBS. It is really important to try not to self-diagnose IBS, or any other condition, as they can all have different causes and different treatments. To make sure you are on the correct path for your symptom management, a proper diagnosis via a medical doctor is recommended. If you suspect you have IBS or an adverse reaction to foods, you should seek the advice of a medical practitioner, such as your GP, a gastroenterologist, an immunologist or an Accredited Practising Dietitian and discuss your symptoms.

Symptoms associated with IBS

Symptoms commonly associated with IBS are listed below. Please note, all of us can experience some of these symptoms from time to time, that is normal. However when the symptoms are occurring frequently, over a significant period of time (e.g. a few months) it is recommended to speak to your doctor about them, and request to start some investigations as to the cause.

- Changes in bowel habits (diarrhoea or constipation or a combination of both)
- Abdominal pain or discomfort
- Excessive flatulence
- Abdominal bloating (feeling of fullness)
- Abdominal distension (abdomen increases in size, a look of being pregnant)
- Reflux/heartburn
- Nausea
- Vomiting (less common)
- Fatigue, weakness, lethargy

CONSULTING WITH A SPECIALIST DIETITIAN

Once you have a diagnosis of IBS, you should seek specific advice about modifying your diet from a qualified dietitian. Many possible food components can contribute to a food intolerance and symptoms of IBS, so it is recommended that you be assessed by an Accredited Practising Dietitian specialising in food intolerances.

Never trial a gluten-free diet to relieve your symptoms until you've been investigated for coeliac disease, as this type of diet can interfere with obtaining accurate results (for more see Coeliac disease below).

A dietitian may determine whether you have an intolerance by taking a dietary history. Before your appointment, it's wise to keep a record of the food you eat in a typical week, and the symptoms you experience during those seven days. This is called a 'seven-day food and symptom diary' – see page 32.

Once you have a diagnosis, an Accredited Practising Dietitian will provide expert advice on which foods to limit and what to replace them with. (You can find an experienced Accredited Practising Dietitian at my practice, Shepherd Works, and we offer Skype and/or telephone consultations for people living interstate or overseas. Find out more by visiting my website www.shepherdworks.com.au.)

Once you know your food triggers you'll need to restrict foods containing the problematic ingredients and become a careful reader of food ingredient labels (see page 63). Good food planning and preparation are vital in ensuring you meet your nutritional needs and avoid unwanted abdominal distress. The severity of symptoms varies; some will need to avoid the problematic food completely, while others may only need to reduce their dietary intake. When you cut out problematic foods, you need to replace them with healthy alternatives to avoid nutritional deficiency and poor health. A dietitian can assist you to make sure you don't miss out on important nutrients.

COELIAC DISEASE

Coeliac disease is estimated to affect one in 60 women and one in 80 men in Australia. It is a medical condition of intolerance to dietary gluten. Gluten is the protein component of wheat, rye and barley (and, in some countries, is considered to be present in oats), and is found in derivatives of these, including triticale and malt. (Note that because gluten is a protein, it is not a FODMAP, all of which are carbohydrates.) In people with coeliac disease, gluten causes an immune reaction that damages the small protrusions on the lining of the small intestine (the villi), flattening them and dramatically decreasing the ability of the intestine to absorb nutrients from food. Coeliac disease is not a food allergy.

There's currently no cure for coeliac disease. The only treatment is a lifelong strict gluten-free diet (even if symptoms are mild or there are no symptoms at all). It's not a trendy, 'fad' diet, but rather a real medical therapy for a real medical condition. A gluten-free diet is more restrictive and excludes more foods than a wheat-free diet. Regular bread, pasta, cereals, cakes, biscuits, pizza, pastry, breadcrumbs, and so on are all obvious gluten sources, but it can also be hidden in many foods, including commercially prepared condiments and sauces, gravies, confectionery, smallgoods and even beer!

Symptoms of coeliac disease range from none at all to the following gastrointestinal symptoms, all of varying severity:

- diarrhoea and/or constipation
- fatigue, weakness and lethargy
- weight loss and in children failure to grow
- flatulence
- abdominal distension and bloating
- cramping
- nausea and vomiting
- reflux (heartburn)
- nutritional deficiencies (in iron, folate, vitamin B12, zinc and vitamin D).

Because these symptoms are quite similar to those of IBS, it's extremely important that anyone who has them be investigated for coeliac disease *before* removing gluten from their diet. Even if you have been told you have, say, fructose malabsorption, that doesn't mean you can't *also* have coeliac disease. Coeliac disease should be investigated in all people with these symptoms.

The tests for coeliac disease include blood test screening, but the gold standard remains a small intestine biopsy. A gene test (performed as a blood test) can be helpful to exclude coeliac disease, since only people with the genes HLA DQ-2 or HLA DQ-8 can develop coeliac disease. If you *do* have either of these genes, this doesn't guarantee that you'll get coeliac disease – one third of the population carries one or both of these genes, but only about 1–2 per cent of the population actually develops coeliac disease.

The reason you should never trial a strict gluten-free diet is that if you actually have coeliac disease, a proper diagnosis won't be possible as your small bowel may already have begun to repair itself as a result of the gluten-free diet. People being investigated for coeliac disease still need to be consuming gluten in their diet.

It is also worthwhile noting that just like asthma and diabetes are two different conditions that can occur in the same person, so too, coeliac disease and IBS can occur in the same person. If you have been diagnosed with coeliac disease and are strictly compliant with your gluten-free diet but still experience symptoms, you may have IBS. Consult with a dietitian with experience in coeliac disease, who will first check your diet for any accidental gluten intake, and if necessary, will teach you how to do a combined gluten-free and Low-FODMAP Diet to manage your coeliac disease and possible IBS.

Navigating the IBS–Low-FODMAP Diet pathway

There's much greater awareness of the various dietary conditions these days, and diagnosis has been streamlined, but many people are still wrongly or poorly diagnosed, often after spending a great deal of time and money seeing numerous practitioners. For this reason, I've produced this flowchart to give you a good idea of what constitutes an effective and comprehensive approach to your symptoms.

PATIENT PRESENTS WITH IBS SYMPTOMS TO HEALTH PRACTITIONER

↓

'Red flags' such as unexplained weight loss, recent onset of symptoms, blood in stools, raised inflammatory markers identified?

YES → Medical investigations as appropriate → Is patient consuming a gluten-containing diet?

NO ↓

Is patient consuming a gluten-containing diet?

NO → Patient must undergo a gluten challenge, i.e. consume 4 slices wheat bread a day for 6 weeks → Undertake medical investigations for coeliac disease

YES ↓

Undertake medical investigations for coeliac disease → Coeliac disease diagnosis positive?

YES →

Appropriate medical management

Referral to a specialist dietitian for education in implementing a strict lifelong gluten-free diet

Referral to Coeliac Australia (coeliac society)

NO ↓

Referral to a specialist gastrointestinal dietitian educated in the Low-FODMAP Diet, and advised to reduce any obvious excesses, such as caffeine, alcohol and fat, if these are likely triggers.

Referral to psychologist and/or hypnotherapist if suitable

↓

Have symptoms improved satisfactorily after following the Low-FODMAP Diet properly for 6–8 weeks?

YES →

Under the guidance of the specialist dietitian, undertake step 2 of the Low-FODMAP Diet i.e. the reintroduction and liberalisation of foods containing FODMAPs as tolerated. This is important to optimise variety in food choices while maintaining symptom control.

Also address nutritional adequacy

NO ↓

Based on degree of symptom change (if at all), under the guidance of the specialist dietitian, manipulate dietary restrictions to identify other culprit foods/food molecules, e.g. a trial food-chemical elimination diet, or gluten-free diet alone or in combination with the Low-FODMAP Diet

↓

Have symptoms improved satisfactorily?

NO ↓

Dietitian and doctor liaise and explain that IBS symptoms may not be caused by diet alone (or at all), and explain gastrointestinal physiology and how stress or anxiety affect symptoms. Maintain any useful dietary changes while achieving nutritional adequacy

↓

Consider other medical management

YES ↓

Specialist dietitian reviews symptoms and food intake. Advises how to restrict identified dietary culprits while still achieving nutritional adequacy

WHAT ARE FODMAPS?

FODMAPs are a collection of short-chain carbohydrates (sugars and related molecules) that occur naturally in many foods, and some can also be added to processed foods. Unlike many other sugars, FODMAPs are not absorbed in the small intestine, and then continue their journey through the digestive tract to the large intestine. FODMAPs are then used as a food source by the bacteria that naturally live in the large intestine, producing gas. Additionally, FODMAPs are concentrated sugars (highly osmotic) in the bowel and can draw water into the bowel via osmosis. The increased gas and water in the intestines can make the bowels blow up like a balloon, and can also change the speed at which the bowel muscles work. These effects, in turn, can trigger symptoms including bloating, distension, excess wind, diarrhoea and/or constipation. FODMAPs can indeed trigger all the symptoms of IBS.

The word 'FODMAP' is an acronym that describes a family of poorly absorbed, highly fermentable short-chain carbohydrates (sugars) and sugar alcohols, falling into five main classes. The acronym gives some hint about what happens to these molecules in the digestive tract, and also describes the size of these molecules – some are very short, some are longer. To understand the term, it's important to know that 'saccharide' means sugar, 'oligo' means few, 'di' means two or double, and 'mono' means one or single. Note: not all carbohydrates are FODMAPs.

FODMAPs are a collection of short-chain carbohydrates (sugars and related molecules) that occur naturally in many foods, and some can also be added to processed foods.

FODMAP stands for:

Fermentable – FODMAPs are not absorbed in the small intestine and therefore travel into the large intestine where they can be broken down (fermented as a food source) by the bacteria that reside there.

Oligosaccharides – As 'oligo' means few and 'saccharide' means sugar, it makes sense that oligosaccharides are chains of individual sugars joined together. There are two oligosaccharide FODMAPs: *fructans* and *galacto-oligosaccharides* (GOS).

Disaccharide – This refers to the double sugar *lactose*.

Monosaccharide – This refers to '*excess fructose*', in other words where fructose, a single sugar, is present in foods in amounts greater than glucose, another single sugar.

And

Polyols – These molecules, related to sugars, are called sugar alcohols (although they won't make you intoxicated!), and include *sorbitol, mannitol, maltitol* and *xylitol*. Isomalt and polydextrose act in a similar way.

WHY THE LOW-FODMAP DIET FOR IBS?

The Low-FODMAP Diet is used internationally as a treatment for IBS as it's the most effective diet for managing IBS symptoms. The Low-FODMAP Diet can also help people who suffer from some or all of these symptoms yet haven't been formally diagnosed with IBS by their doctor.

The Low-FODMAP Diet has been embraced by sufferers of digestive symptoms from around the world and is also recommended by doctors because it's backed by scientific evidence:

- We know very clearly that it's FODMAPs that induce symptoms of IBS and not any other molecules in foods.
- We have an excellent understanding of how it is that FODMAPs cause symptoms – it isn't just a fad diet.
- The results in people who've tried the Low-FODMAP Diet to manage their symptoms are more impressive than with any other diet – the Low-FODMAP Diet provides symptom relief in 75 per cent of IBS sufferers.
- The Low-FODMAP Diet can continue to offer symptom relief in the long term. People have continued to follow the diet for many years.
- It's a diet that's effective around the world, as FODMAPs are not unique to Australian food. The diet has been used as an effective therapy for IBS in the United Kingdom, New Zealand, Denmark, Austria, Switzerland, Norway, France and the United States, among other countries.

> *I am so grateful for your research and the results. A Health System dietitian recommended I read about the Low-FODMAP Diet after I presented with what she saw as 'classic' signs of illness and intolerance to every category of carbohydrate in the FODMAP acronym. As a child I recall getting stomach aches from wheat, milk, cookies and, horrors, especially legumes. I was once told I'm allergic to legumes but in recent years have not tested as allergic to peanuts although they make me ill with gastrointestinal symptoms. Now I understand! I've been on the FODMAP eating plan for about four months and feel like a happy bon vivant 61-year-old! I'm a licensed clinical social worker, love what I do and think I have more energy than when I was in my forties.*

PSYCHOLOGICAL ASPECTS

When people are first introduced to the Low-FODMAP Diet and discover foods such as wheat and onion are restricted, the first response is often shock, followed shortly after by disappointment, frustration and often grieving for the foods that are limited. By contrast, however, these negative feelings are often offset by the positive feelings of symptom management, a direct result of the FODMAP modification improving symptoms. For many, the changes are worth the sacrifice of restricted food choices, especially considering the strict restriction is only for 6–8 weeks in most cases (this is described on pages 29–37).

You can 'cheat' on the diet – based on current knowledge, there is no damage caused to the bowels if you should splurge and eat foods that are high in FODMAPs – the worst that will happen is your symptoms will be triggered. It is your choice: if you are tempted by a high FODMAP food, you can weigh up the benefit of eating it versus the impact of the symptoms – sometimes you might think the food tempting you is worth the symptoms!

If you are really having difficulties adjusting, then ensure you talk to your health professional to discuss your feelings. If cutting out all high-FODMAP foods all at once (as is described in Step One of this book) doesn't feel right for you, it might be more manageable and less burdensome for you to take a slower approach, cutting out one FODMAP group at a time over a few weeks, to gradually reach the restriction you need for your symptom relief. This diet is meant to be a positive change for your physical health (IBS symptoms), however if it is causing too much stress, affecting your mental health, then a different approach may be needed for you. I recommend consulting with an experienced dietitian for individualised advice to meet your needs – you can still achieve your goals, it may just be via another route. Gut-focused clinical hypnotherapists (such as at www.shepherdworks.com.au) and other IBS-focused psychologists may also be able to assist. It is important to manage worries as stress, depression and anxiety can all be independent triggers for IBS symptoms.

This book will assist with managing those feelings. It won't take you long to get through Step One, and you'll be through to the reintroduction process, and well into Step Two before you know it, enjoying your own liberalised FODMAP-modified eating plan where you don't have to restrict so much, and you can enjoy a greater variety of foods. This book will help your longer term eating habits by making them as non-restrictive as possible. I firmly believe that.

You can 'cheat' on the diet – based on current knowledge, there is no damage caused to the bowels if you should splurge and eat foods that are high in FODMAPs – the worst that will happen is your symptoms will be triggered.

2. INTRODUCING FODMAPS

As we've seen, there are five main classes of FODMAPs. These are described in greater detail in this chapter, including the foods that are high in each FODMAP. Foods that contain FODMAPs can be split into three categories:

1. Those with *large* amounts of FODMAPs (i.e. the amount consumed in a serve of the food is definitely above the cut-off that has been shown to cause symptoms).
2. Those with *moderate* amounts of FODMAPs (i.e. the amount consumed in a serve of food is elevated, but not excessively so. These foods should be suitable when consumed *up to* the quantities defined in the following tables).
3. Those that are *low* in FODMAPs (i.e. they contain FODMAPs at a level that has been proven to be well tolerated by people with IBS). These foods are listed in the tables on pages 26–27.

Note that we don't look specifically for 'FODMAP-free' foods. (Please refer to table on page 24 – it summarises high-FODMAP foods to be aware of for easy reference.) Acknowledgement to Monash University Central Clinical School, Fodmap Pty Ltd and SSSG International Pty Ltd for the information about FODMAP-tested foods. (The author is not associated with Monash University.)

The Low-FODMAP Diet is used internationally as a treatment for IBS as it's the most effective diet for managing IBS symptoms.

FODMAP 1: EXCESS FRUCTOSE

Fructose is sometimes known as the fruit sugar – it is present in every fruit. There's some good news when it comes to fructose restriction – you don't have to avoid every food that contains fructose, including fruit! Foods that have a balance of fructose and glucose have been shown to be well absorbed in people with fructose malabsorption, as are foods that contain more glucose than fructose, when eaten one serving at a time. Foods are usually only a problem for people with fructose malabsorption if they contain excess fructose (more fructose than glucose).

One method people use to avoid excess fructose is glucose matching, although this approach doesn't have strong scientific evidence to support it. Glucose matching involves consuming enough glucose at the same time as the food containing excess fructose in order to bring the glucose and fructose into balance or to create an excess of glucose.

It's worth noting, however, that balancing fructose with glucose through glucose matching may only be of benefit to people with fructose malabsorption. It won't assist absorption of lactose, GOS, fructans or polyols (as described on pages 18–22). It's also important to note that it will only be of benefit when consuming foods whose *only* problematic FODMAP is excess fructose. In other words, if a food contains excess fructose together with a few other problematic FODMAPs, glucose matching will be of limited benefit, as it will not aid the absorption of the other FODMAPs present, so symptoms are still likely. Glucose matching may therefore assist in eating mango and boysenberries, but it won't work for apples, which also contain sorbitol – the added glucose will balance the fructose, but won't help at all with the sorbitol.

FOODS CONTAINING LARGE AMOUNTS OF EXCESS FRUCTOSE (PER SERVE)

FRUITS AND FRUIT PRODUCTS	VEGETABLES	OTHER
▪ Apples ▪ Boysenberries ▪ Mangoes ▪ Nashi pears ▪ Pears ▪ Tamarillos ▪ Watermelon ▪ Fruit juice concentrate ▪ Fruit juices (apple, pear, mango, tropical)	▪ Artichokes (Jerusalem) ▪ Asparagus ▪ Sugar snap peas	▪ Agave ▪ High-fructose corn syrup ▪ Honey

FOODS CONTAINING MODERATE AMOUNTS OF EXCESS FRUCTOSE (PER SERVE)

FRUITS AND FRUIT PRODUCTS	VEGETABLES	OTHER
▪ Cherries – up to 3 fresh	—	—

FRUCTOSE LOAD

The first key to managing the FODMAP of excess fructose is to choose fruit in which glucose and fructose are in balance or there is more glucose than fructose. It's also important to note, however, that you should limit the number of these 'balanced' fruits you eat at one time. When choosing a 'balanced' fruit (see the table on page 26), eat only the equivalent of one serve of fruit (e.g. one piece of fruit) at a time. This ensures you don't have an excessive fructose load, which can trigger symptoms even if the fruit is in balance. Some examples of suitable 'serves' of fruit include:

- *1 whole banana or orange*
- *2 kiwifruit or mandarins*
- *1 small slice of rockmelon, honeydew melon or pineapple*
- *1 small handful of strawberries, blueberries, raspberries or grapes*
- *⅓–½ glass of suitable juice (e.g. orange juice, not apple or pear juice)*
- *1 tablespoon dried fruit*

This advice doesn't mean you can only have one piece of fruit per day. On the contrary, you can enjoy many pieces of 'balanced' fruit if you wish, as long as you wait 2–3 hours after eating some 'balanced' fruit before you have your next serve.

FODMAP 2: LACTOSE

Lactose is known as the milk sugar as it is present in the milk from any mammal – cow, sheep, goat, buffalo – even human! A common misconception with lactose malabsorption (i.e. lactose intolerance) is that you need to cut out every single trace of lactose from your diet. This is quite wrong – small amounts of lactose-containing foods are often tolerated. In fact, most people with lactose intolerance can tolerate up to 4 grams of lactose per sitting. To put this in perspective, one glass of milk contains 12–16 grams of lactose, so while a whole glass of milk isn't good, a splash in tea or coffee will be less than 4 grams and will be fine for most lactose-intolerant people.

Also, milk and milk products need not be completely withdrawn from the diet, as not every product made from milk contains lactose (hard cheeses, for example, are virtually lactose-free, as indicated in the table on page 26). Although it may be ideal to choose low-lactose and lactose-free products whenever possible, there's good news when it comes to your favourite high-lactose foods and drinks. You can purchase the lactase enzyme (the 'scissors' that break down lactose so it can be absorbed) in tablet form from pharmacies. Instructions are on the packet, but the general rule is the more lactose in the food you're consuming, the more tablets you need – in other words, it's dose-related. You need to take the lactase tablets at the same time you consume the lactose-containing food for them to work effectively.

> "*I have Crohn's and as a result have had a total colectomy. For five years I have had all kinds of trouble with gas and output via my stoma. Your diet has solved it – I really wish that I had known about your diet while I still had a colon because I do not think my Crohn's would have been so terribly painful and quite so debilitating. Thank you so much.*
>
> *I am, however, more grateful for the impact on my 21-year-old daughter's life. All through her teenage years she has had terrible trouble with pain, bloating, nausea and the trots. We had her tested because I was terrified she had Crohn's. She doesn't have any inflammatory bowel disease – there was an unconvinced diagnosis of possible IBS.*
>
> *I FODMAP'd her diet and the massive improvement in the quality of my daughter's life is tremendous and just in time for her going to uni. She no longer spends 90 minutes in the bathroom every morning or bloats, etc. It removes the unpredictability of her guts. Having eliminated the FODMAP group of symptoms we have also been able to identify that she is lactose-intolerant. She is a different girl and at last has the chance to reach her full potential and also enjoy life. I am so very very grateful to you, Dr Shepherd – in our house you are a goddess.*
>
> *Thank you!!!*"

FOODS CONTAINING LARGE AMOUNTS OF LACTOSE (PER SERVE)

MILK AND MILK PRODUCTS	OTHER
■ Milk – cow's, sheep's, goat's (full-fat, low-fat, skim) ■ Custard ■ Dairy desserts ■ Evaporated milk ■ Ice cream ■ Milk powder ■ Sweetened condensed milk	—

FOODS CONTAINING MODERATE AMOUNTS OF LACTOSE (PER SERVE)

MILK AND MILK PRODUCTS	OTHER
■ Yoghurt – cow's, sheep's, goat's (full-fat, low-fat, skim) – up to 80 grams (⅓ cup) ■ Soft cheeses – cottage, ricotta, quark, cream cheese, mascarpone, crème fraîche – up to 2 tablespoons	■ Regular milk in tea and coffee – up to ¼ cup ■ Regular milk or milk powder in baked foods such as cakes – up to 1 large serve of cake ■ Regular milk or milk powder in chocolate – up to 40 grams milk chocolate

FODMAP 3: POLYOLS

Polyols are a group of sugar alcohols. They tend to end in the suffix -ol, but isomalt and polydextrose should also be considered part of the polyol group as they have a polyol component. Two types of polyols occur naturally in foods: sorbitol and mannitol. These, along with the other polyols (xylitol, maltitol and polyol-related molecules of isomalt and polydextrose), can also be used as food additives. If they are, the package will have a warning statement on the food product: 'WARNING: Excess consumption may have a laxative effect.' Besides this effect, these polyols are potent wind-generators and major bloaters! If polyols are used as additives, their name or additive number may be listed in the ingredients list, as outlined in the following table. (Please also see page 62.)

POLYOL	ADDITIVE NUMBER (ON INGREDIENTS LIST)
Isomalt (contains sorbitol and mannitol)	953
Maltitol	965
Mannitol	421
Polydextrose (10% sorbitol)	1200
Sorbitol	420
Xylitol	967

Erythritol, although a polyol is not as potent in triggering symptoms as other polyols and is usually tolerated by many with IBS when consumed in moderate amounts. Assess individual tolerance.

Sorbitol

FOODS CONTAINING LARGE AMOUNTS OF SORBITOL (PER SERVE)

FRUITS AND FRUIT PRODUCTS	VEGETABLES
■ Apples ■ Apricots (fresh and dried) ■ Blackberries ■ Coconut water ■ Nashi pears ■ Nectarines ■ Peaches ■ Pears ■ Plums	–

FOODS CONTAINING MODERATE AMOUNTS OF SORBITOL (PER SERVE)

FRUITS AND FRUIT PRODUCTS	VEGETABLES
■ Cherries – up to 3 fresh ■ Longon – up to 10 ■ Lychee – up to 5	

Mannitol

FOODS CONTAINING LARGE AMOUNTS OF MANNITOL (PER SERVE)

FRUITS AND FRUIT PRODUCTS	VEGETABLES
▪ Watermelon	▪ Cauliflower ▪ Mushrooms

FOODS CONTAINING MODERATE AMOUNTS OF MANNITOL (PER SERVE)

FRUITS AND FRUIT PRODUCTS	VEGETABLES
–	▪ Butternut pumpkin – up to ½ cup ▪ Celery – up to ½ stick

FODMAP 4: FRUCTANS

Fructans are a FODMAP in everyone – it's just a matter of how much we need to consume before we experience symptoms. The main food sources of fructans are some vegetables, grains, nuts and fruits, as shown in the table below. You will notice wheat, rye and barley are listed. People with IBS tend to experience symptoms when consuming large serves of wheat, rye and/or barley. Not every wheat-, rye- or barley-based ingredient needs to be avoided, however – only large amounts such as in the foods listed in the table. The good news is that small amounts of wheat are usually well tolerated, such as the amount in a chocolate-coated wafer, or soy sauce, for example.

FOODS CONTAINING LARGE AMOUNTS OF FRUCTANS (PER SERVE)

FRUITS AND FRUIT PRODUCTS	VEGETABLES	GRAIN- AND STARCH-BASED FOODS	NUTS AND SEEDS	OTHER
▪ Custard apples ▪ Nectarines ▪ Persimmons ▪ Watermelon	▪ Artichokes – globe ▪ Artichokes – Jerusalem ▪ Garlic ▪ Leeks ▪ Onions ▪ Shallots ▪ Spring onions (white part only)	▪ Barley (in large amounts) ▪ Rye (in large amounts) ▪ Spelt (in large amounts) ▪ Wheat (in large amounts) ▪ Barley-, rye- and wheat-based bread, pasta, couscous, gnocchi, noodles, croissants, muffins, crumpets	▪ Cashews ▪ Pistachios	▪ Additives: inulin, fructo-oligosaccharides ▪ Chickpeas ▪ Chicory-based drinks ▪ Legumes (e.g. red kidney beans) ▪ Lentils (but cooking and draining lowers FODMAP content) ▪ Salts – onion, garlic, chicken, vegetable

FOODS CONTAINING MODERATE AMOUNTS OF FRUCTANS (PER SERVE)

FRUITS AND FRUIT PRODUCTS	VEGETABLES	GRAIN- AND STARCH-BASED FOODS	NUTS AND SEEDS	OTHER
■ Rambutans – up to 4 fresh ■ Pomegranates – up to ¼ cup seeds	■ Beetroot – up to 2 slices	■ Crackers – up to 3 ■ Plain sweet biscuits – up to 3	■ Hazelnuts – up to 10 ■ Tahini – up to 1 tablespoon	—

FODMAP 5: GALACTO-OLIGOSACCHARIDES (GOS)

GOS are predominantly found in the legume family, including chickpeas and lentils. These are important foods for vegetarians (especially vegans), as they contain significant amounts of protein. (See page 39 if you're a vegetarian following a Low-FODMAP Diet.)

FOODS CONTAINING LARGE AMOUNTS OF GALACTO-OLIGOSACCHARIDES (PER SERVE)

LEGUMES AND LEGUME PRODUCTS	NUTS
■ Chickpeas ■ Hummus ■ Legumes – red kidney beans, baked beans, borlotti beans, soybeans, navy beans, butter beans, etc. ■ Lentils (but cooking and draining lowers FODMAP content) ■ Refried beans ■ Soy milk (made from *whole* soybeans)	■ Cashews ■ Pistachios

FOODS CONTAINING MODERATE AMOUNTS OF GALACTO-OLIGOSACCHARIDES (PER SERVE)

VEGETABLES	NUTS
■ Beetroot – up to 2 slices ■ Butternut pumpkin – up to ½ cup ■ Sweetcorn – up to ½ cob ■ Green peas – up to ¼ cup	■ Almonds – up to 10 ■ Hazelnuts – up to 10

EXAMPLES OF FOODS HIGH IN FODMAPS (PER SERVE)

FRUIT AND FRUIT PRODUCTS	VEGETABLES	MILK AND MILK PRODUCTS
■ Apples ■ Apricots (fresh and dried) ■ Blackberries ■ Boysenberries ■ Cherries – more than 3 fresh ■ Coconut water ■ Custard apples ■ Dried fruit – more than 1 tablespoon ■ Fruit juice concentrate ■ Fruit juice – apple, pear, mango, tropical ■ Longans – more than 10 ■ Lychees – more than 5 ■ Mangoes ■ Nashi pears ■ Nectarines ■ Peaches ■ Pears ■ Persimmons ■ Plums ■ Pomegranates – more than ¼ cup seeds ■ Rambutans – more than 4 fresh ■ Tamarillos ■ Watermelon	■ Artichokes – globe ■ Artichokes – Jerusalem ■ Asparagus ■ Beetroot – more than 2 slices ■ Butternut pumpkin – more than ½ cup ■ Cauliflower ■ Celery – more than ½ stick ■ Garlic ■ Green peas – more than ¼ cup ■ Leek ■ Mushrooms ■ Onions ■ Shallots ■ Spring onions (white part only) ■ Sugar snap peas ■ Sweetcorn – more than ½ cob	■ Cow's milk (full-fat, low-fat, skim) ■ Custard ■ Dairy desserts ■ Evaporated milk ■ Goat's milk (full-fat, low-fat, skim) ■ Ice cream ■ Milk powder ■ Regular milk in tea and coffee – more than ¼ cup ■ Regular milk or milk powder in baked foods – more than 1 large serve of cake ■ Regular milk or milk powder in chocolate – more than 25 grams milk chocolate ■ Sheep's milk (full-fat, low-fat, skim) ■ Soft cheeses – cottage, ricotta, quark, cream cheese, mascarpone, crème fraîche – more than 2 tablespoons ■ Soy milk (from whole soybeans) ■ Sweetened condensed milk ■ Yoghurt – cow's, sheep's, goat's (full-fat, low-fat, skim) – more than ⅓ cup

GRAIN AND STARCH FOODS

- Barley (in large amounts)
- Barley-, rye- and wheat-based commercial bread, bread crumbs, breakfast cereals, muesli, pasta, couscous, gnocchi, noodles, pastries, cakes, biscuits, croissants, muffins, crumpets, spaetzle
- Flours (in large amounts) including chickpea flour (besan), lentil flour, pea flour, soy flour
- Plain sweet biscuits – more than 3
- Rye (in large amounts)
- Spelt (in large amounts) in bread (except some sourdough varieties), pasta, cereals
- Wheat (in large amounts) including bulgar, durum, wheat flour, multigrain flour, triticale, wheatgerm, wheat bran, semolina
- Wheat-based crackers, crispbreads – more than 3

OTHERS

- Agave
- Almonds – more than 10
- Cashews
- Chickpeas
- Chicory-based drinks
- Chutneys – many varieties
- Dessert wines – many varieties
- Fructo-oligosaccharides
- Hazelnuts – more than 10
- High-fructose corn syrup
- Honey
- Hummus
- Inulin
- Legumes – red kidney beans, soybeans, borlotti beans, refried beans, etc.
- Lentils (note: cooking and draining lowers FODMAP content)
- Onion-containing gravies
- Pistachios
- Relishes – many varieties
- Salts – onion, garlic, vegetable, chicken
- Sausages – many types (check for onion and dehydrated vegetable powder)
- Some rums
- Stock cubes – many varieties
- Sweeteners – sorbitol (420), mannitol (421), xylitol (967), maltitol (965), isomalt (953), polydextrose (1200)
- Tahini – more than 1 tablespoon

EXAMPLES OF FOODS LOW IN FODMAPS (PER SERVE)

FRUIT AND FRUIT PRODUCTS	VEGETABLES	MILK AND MILK PRODUCTS
▪ Avocados ▪ Bananas ▪ Blueberries ▪ Cantaloupe ▪ Carambolas ▪ Coconut cream ▪ Coconut milk ▪ Dragonfruit ▪ Durian ▪ Grapes ▪ Honeydew melon ▪ Kiwifruit ▪ Lemons ▪ Limes ▪ Mandarins ▪ Oranges ▪ Passionfruit ▪ Pawpaw ▪ Pineapple ▪ Raspberries ▪ Rhubarb ▪ Strawberries ▪ Tangelos	▪ Alfalfa ▪ Bamboo shoots ▪ Bean sprouts ▪ Beans (green) ▪ Bok choy ▪ Broccoli ▪ Capsicum ▪ Carrots ▪ Chives ▪ Choy sum ▪ Cucumber ▪ Eggplant ▪ Endive ▪ Fennel bulb ▪ Ginger ▪ Kale ▪ Kohlrabi ▪ Lettuce ▪ Olives ▪ Parsnips ▪ Potatoes ▪ Radicchio ▪ Radishes ▪ Rocket ▪ Seaweed (nori) ▪ Silverbeet ▪ Spinach ▪ Spring onions (green part only) ▪ Squash ▪ Swedes ▪ Sweet potato ▪ Tomatoes ▪ Turnips ▪ Water chestnuts ▪ Zucchini	▪ Blue vein cheese ▪ Bocconcini ▪ Brie ▪ Butter ▪ Cheddar ▪ Chocolate containing regular milk or powdered milk – a nibble ▪ Colby ▪ Cream (lactose-free cream is also available) ▪ Edam ▪ Feta ▪ Gloucester cheese ▪ Gorgonzola ▪ Gouda ▪ Gruyère ▪ Havarti ▪ Lactose-free ice cream ▪ Lactose-free yoghurt ▪ Margarine ▪ Mozzarella ▪ Neufchatel ▪ Oat milk – most varieties ▪ Parmesan ▪ Pecorino ▪ Raclette ▪ Regular milk in tea and coffee – a splash of milk ▪ Rice milk – most varieties ▪ Soft cheeses – cottage, ricotta, quark, cream cheese, mascarpone, crème fraîche – a spoonful ▪ Swiss cheese ▪ Taleggio ▪ Yoghurt – cow's, sheep's, goat's (full-fat, low-fat, skim) – a spoonful or two

GRAIN AND STARCH FOODS	OTHERS
■ Arrowroot ■ Buckwheat ■ Corn ■ Custard Powder ■ Gluten-free biscuits, cakes, pastries, rice cakes ■ Gluten-free bread and cereal products ■ Gluten-free pasta, rice noodles, rice vermicelli, soba noodles (100 per cent buckwheat), mung bean (glass) noodles ■ Gluten-free taco shells, maize tortillas ■ Gnocchi (small amount of wheat tolerated) ■ Malt ■ Millet, puffed millet ■ Oat bran ■ Oats, rolled oats ■ Plain wheat biscuits – up to 3 ■ Polenta ■ Quinoa ■ Rice (white, brown) – ground rice, rice bran, glutinous rice, wild rice ■ Rice- or corn-based fruit-free breakfast cereals, baby rice cereal, porridge ■ Sorghum ■ Some spelt sourdough breads ■ Wheat-based crackers – up to 3 ■ Flour – cornmeal, maize cornflour, potato flour, rice flour, sago, tapioca, oatmeal (For more detail on flours etc., see the table on page 66)	■ Alcohol – most (see page 92) ■ Almonds – up to 10 ■ Baking powder ■ Bicarbonate of soda ■ Chia seeds ■ Cocoa ■ Garlic-infused olive oil ■ Gelatine ■ Hazelnuts – up to 10 ■ Herbs (see page 91) ■ Honey substitutes: maple syrup, golden syrup ■ Jam, marmalade ■ Linseed (flaxseed) ■ Meat, fish, chicken, eggs, tofu – plain ■ Onion-infused olive oil ■ Peanut butter ■ Poppy seeds ■ Pumpkin seeds (pepitas) ■ Pure icing sugar ■ Salt ■ Sesame seeds ■ Soft drink ■ Soy sauce ■ Spices (see page 91) ■ Sugar (sucrose), glucose, stevia, any other artificial sweeteners not ending in '-ol' (e.g. aspartame) ■ Sunflower seeds ■ Tahini – up to 1 tablespoon ■ Tamari ■ Tea, coffee ■ Vinegar ■ Water, mineral water, soda water, tonic water ■ Xanthan gum

3. A TWO-STEP PLAN FOR IMPLEMENTING THE LOW-FODMAP DIET

Now you have read the first two chapters, you should feel comfortable in your understanding about what FODMAPs are, the foods they are found in, and how they can trigger symptoms of IBS. The Low-FODMAP Diet has been embraced around the world and it is likely you will meet more and more people following the diet as time passes. This chapter will teach you how you, too, can follow the diet.

Interestingly, the Low-FODMAP Diet differs to other diets used to manage adverse reactions to food, such as coeliac disease and allergies. For example, a gluten-free diet for coeliac disease involves the strict restriction of all gluten (even crumbs!) for life – no 'breaking' the diet! For those with anaphylactic allergy to nuts, it is important not to break the diet either, as there can be dire life-threatening consequences. These are examples of diets that require strict avoidance – a little bit of problematic foods is not okay.

By contrast, the Low-FODMAP Diet has a lot of flexibility. This is a dietary management that is tailored just for you! People following the Low-FODMAP Diet will all have different needs. To help determine your needs, undertake the two-step process described. You will typically find that a small amount of foods containing FODMAPs is indeed alright, and you may find that you can tolerate more than just a little (it is a Low-FODMAP Diet, not a NO-FODMAP diet!). You may also find you don't have a problem with every type of FODMAP – in fact many people find that while some types of FODMAPs are definite triggers for their symptoms, other types of FODMAPs can be well tolerated. Everyone is different.

There's simply no point restricting more foods than you need to in order to feel well.

Here are some suggestions on how to embark on your two-step Low-FODMAP Diet journey. It is recommended to undertake both Step One and Step Two in consultation with an experienced dietitian.

> "*After many years of various tests, several dietitians, sleepless nights and not least intolerable pain, my boyfriend finally discovered the Low-FODMAP Diet. He has only been on it for one to two weeks so far but we are both noticing a huge difference. He is not in as much pain, he can sleep without waking up in the middle of the night due to a painful stomach and I have got my boyfriend back!*"

STEP ONE: THE STRICT PHASE

SUMMARY OF STEP ONE

- *Aim is to identify if FODMAPs are triggers for IBS symptoms.*
- *Restrict foods high in all or selected FODMAPs for six to eight weeks.*
- *Monitor improvement – this should usually be seen within two weeks, with ongoing improvement in the following weeks.*

Identifying which FODMAPs cause your IBS symptoms

The aim of Step One is to investigate if FODMAPs are triggers for your IBS symptoms. This is usually done by restricting foods known to be high in all FODMAPs for six to eight weeks. This broad approach is suggested as, although many people don't have their symptoms triggered by every type of FODMAP, it can be hard to know which ones are your triggers as you commence this first step of your low-FODMAP journey.

You may be able to work out which FODMAPs are the most likely triggers for your symptoms, especially with the help of an experienced dietitian. This is best done by keeping a seven-day food and symptom diary (see page 32) ...

If you're like many people and eat a variety of foods, then the culprits could be dispersed throughout your diet and it won't necessarily be clear which one is the trigger. In such instances, it's often most practical to cut out all FODMAPs from your diet for six to eight weeks, as it can be the fastest pathway to symptom relief.

You may be able to work out which FODMAPs are the most likely triggers for your symptoms, especially with the help of an experienced dietitian (see resources on page 274). This is best done by keeping a seven-day food and symptom diary (see page 32) and looking out for a relationship between the frequency and severity of your symptoms and the foods you ate anytime earlier in the day. Consume and record your usual diet – the food and drink you usually consume when you experience your IBS symptoms. Through asking you some specific questions and looking at a completed seven-day food and symptom diary, your dietitian may establish that you seem to tolerate one or more types of FODMAPs. For example, the information that your dietitian gathers may indicate you can tolerate milk. If you can, then lactose may not be a problem for you. It is wise to look at the list of foods high in lactose and be sure that none of these trigger symptoms in you. If you and your dietitian are confident lactose is not your problem, then it may be decided that lactose does not need to be restricted in Step One.

Although some individualisation in the first step is possible (such as the lactose example described above), the more common approach is to restrict foods in all types of FODMAPs. Try the Step One menu plans on pages 40–47 to help guide you to delicious eating while restricting all FODMAPs.

This first step highlights the role FODMAPs play in triggering your symptoms. The goal of this step is for you to attain relief with your IBS symptoms by restricting high-FODMAP foods from your diet. It's then important to have a review appointment with a dietitian to assess your symptom response and begin Step Two.

> *"You may recall in late December 2011, we were in search of your Low-FODMAP Diet book which you recommended. We did however manage to find one here in the UK. The book has made thinking about food, and what not to eat, a whole lot better. She [My wife] has improved out of sight."*

A SEVEN-DAY FOOD AND SYMPTOM DIARY

Please record all food and drinks consumed, brand names can be helpful. Please also indicate any gastrointestinal symptoms and the time you experience them.

NAME: ....

DIARY START DATE: ....

	BREAKFAST	MID-MORNING	LUNCH
MONDAY			
TUESDAY			
WEDNESDAY			
THURSDAY			
FRIDAY			
SATURDAY			
SUNDAY			

AFTERNOON	DINNER	SUPPER	SYMPTOMS

STEP TWO: REINTRODUCTION AND LIBERALISATION

SUMMARY OF STEP TWO

- *Liberalise your diet so that it's not unnecessarily restricted.*
- *Eat a greater variety of foods while maintaining symptom control.*
- *Commence this step in consultation with your dietitian, ideally at your review appointment, after assessing your symptom response to the strict phase (Step One).*
- *Reintroduce FODMAPs in a controlled way with foods that contain only one type of FODMAP at a time.*
- *Learn which FODMAPs you can include by exploring: first, whether you can tolerate a whole FODMAP group that you previously cut out; and secondly, whether you can tolerate larger serves of foods containing these FODMAPs.*
- *Determine the* types *and* amounts *of FODMAPS you can tolerate while still enjoying symptom relief.*

It is now time to assess how well your symptoms have improved after the first six to eight weeks doing Step One. You (and your dietitian at your review appointment) can now evaluate how symptoms have changed since you commenced the diet. For help finding a dietitian, see the resources on page 274. If your symptoms have had a noticeable, satisfactory improvement, then it is time to follow a plan to reintroduce foods slowly, in a structured individualised way, to determine types and amounts of FODMAPs you can tolerate.

There's simply no point restricting more foods than you need to in order to feel well. Although Step One is important to determine if FODMAPs are triggers for your symptoms, it's usually more restrictive than necessary for you to achieve symptom relief. It's much better to eat a greater variety of foods and feel just as well as when you were eating less variety in Step One. Additionally, FODMAPs are like prebiotics; restricting all FODMAPs may change the amount and type of bacteria in your large intestine. Any FODMAPs you can tolerate are good for other aspects of your bowel health.

First, a reminder of some key FODMAP facts:

- All people with IBS have different FODMAP tolerance levels.
- Not everyone has a problem with every type of FODMAP.
- Symptoms are due to a dose response, and the dose that is tolerated differs from person to person, which means that increased amounts of some FODMAPs may be tolerated in some people.

So the aim of Step Two is to liberalise your food intake so that your diet is not unnecessarily restricted. It is recommended to work with your dietitian so they can show how to include a greater variety of foods in your diet while maintaining the symptom control you achieved in Step One.

It's not desirable to completely restrict all high-FODMAP foods forever. It's preferable that you work out:

- which FODMAPs are a problem for you (as not everyone has a problem with all FODMAPs), and
- how much of particular high-FODMAP foods you can handle before you get symptoms (everyone has a different tolerance threshold).

This is done via a plan to reintroduce foods slowly, one FODMAP at a time in a structured way so you can establish your own individualised FODMAP-modified dietary needs.

Reintroduce FODMAPs in a controlled way to determine the types and amounts of FODMAPs you can tolerate while still enjoying symptom relief.

How to do a FODMAP challenge

Each week, test a new FODMAP using the suggestions on page 37. The foods suggested contain only one FODMAP. Consume that food three times in the test week in the amount specified. You don't need to eat it every day. The purpose is to see if you can handle the food in the suggested quantity, at a 'normal' frequency in the diet, without pushing yourself. (Too much of anything can potentially cause symptoms in anyone!)

In summary:

- Each week try a new FODMAP challenge (in the order suggested opposite).
- Keep your alcohol and caffeine intake consistent (and any other foods that don't agree with you).
- Eat the recommended test food in the recommended quantity.
- Eat the food three times in the test week (cease if symptoms triggered), included in a meal if suitable (i.e. you don't have to eat ½ cup raw mushrooms on its own!).
- Each time, assess any symptoms you develop after eating it:
- Record the food you have eaten and any symptoms you experience in a record sheet, similar to the example shown on page 36.
    - **If you don't get symptoms**, keep that food in your diet and move on to the next FODMAP group the following week.
    - **If you do get symptoms**, , assume that type of FODMAP is a problem and continue to restrict foods high in this FODMAP, or:
        - You might like to try again with only half the amount you originally tried, to see if you can tolerate a smaller quantity of foods containing this FODMAP, or
        - You may wish to try another food from within the same FODMAP group to confirm the sensitivity.

- Remember to wait until you're symptom-free then move on to the next FODMAP challenge.

The Step Two menu plans on pages 48–59 will help you with reintroducing lactose, sorbitol, excess fructose, fructans and GOS (with some fructan tolerance too, as most foods with GOS in them also have fructans).

WEEK: ....

FOOD EATEN: ....

	SYMPTOMS
DAY 1	
DAY 2	
DAY 3	
ADDITIONAL COMMENTS	

FODMAPs and your diet in the longer term

Now that you have completed all of the reintroductions for the FODMAP groups you restricted in Step One, you are aware of the types and amounts of FODMAPs that are your symptom triggers.

You can now include other foods that contain the FODMAPs that you tolerated in your reintroduction trial into your diet again. Refer to pages 17–22 to see the other foods that contain the FODMAPs you now tolerate, and enjoy them as tolerated. Note that if your symptoms return, it may be due to the accumulation of different FODMAPs (e.g. having an additive effect) as well as large doses of individual FODMAPs. Also be aware that your sensitivity to FODMAPs may change over time, so it is recommended to try reintroducing any failed FODMAP again in the future.

EIGHT-WEEK FODMAP CHALLENGE

CHALLENGE WEEK ONE – MANNITOL

½ cup mushrooms or
⅓ cup cauliflower

CHALLENGE WEEK TWO – SORBITOL

2 fresh apricots or
4 apricot halves (dried or tinned, drained)

CHALLENGE WEEK THREE – LACTOSE

½ cup low-fat milk or
200 gram tub plain low-fat yoghurt

CHALLENGE WEEK FOUR – EXCESS FRUCTOSE

3 teaspoons honey or
1 mango cheek

CHALLENGE WEEK FIVE – FRUCTANS A*

2 slices wholemeal bread

CHALLENGE WEEK SIX – FRUCTANS B*

1 clove garlic or
½ cup leek (white and green sections)

CHALLENGE WEEK SEVEN – FRUCTANS C*

¼ cup onion

CHALLENGE WEEK EIGHT – GALACTO-OLIGOSACCHARIDES

½ cup cooked drained legumes
e.g. red kidney beans or lentils

* A wide range of foods contain fructans, in varying amounts. So the fructan challenge is staggered over three levels, increasing in the amount of fructans at each level from A to C. This is helpful to show that in someone who passes fructan challenge A and B but doesn't tolerate challenge C, it doesn't have to mean all fructan-containing foods need to be restricted – foods that are the equivalent of levels A and B should be tolerated.

Fructan Level A equivalents: dry biscuits, crackers, rye bread, barley bread, spelt pasta
Fructan Level B equivalents:

- Use a whole onion or baby onions in soups, gravies or casseroles etc., and remove prior to serving.
- Cut onion into large chunks in stir fries, sauces, risottos etc. and leave behind on plate.

Also, remember several foods contain more than one FODMAP. For example, apples contain both excess fructose and sorbitol. If you found during the reintroduction process that you can tolerate more than one FODMAP, you can trial your tolerance to foods that contain the FODMAPs that you tolerated. So if you can tolerate excess fructose and sorbitol, then you may now like to trial your tolerance to apples.

WHAT IF THE LOW-FODMAP DIET DOESN'T WORK FOR ME?

The Low-FODMAP Diet doesn't cure IBS, rather it is an effective treatment to minimise symptoms. It works effectively to make IBS symptoms manageable in the majority of people who try it. Around 75–80% of those who go on the Low-FODMAP Diet are happy with their symptom response, as shown through many of the real life testimonials in this book. However, if you try the Low-FODMAP Diet and it does not adequately manage your symptoms, you may be wondering what to do next. Your symptoms could be triggered by other foods or food components including alcohol, fat, caffeine, gluten, or natural food chemicals including salicylates, amines and glutamates. If you are confident that foods trigger your symptoms, consult with a gastro-intestinal specialist dietitian to explore further the relationship between your food and symptoms.

Although food seems to be the logical trigger for IBS symptoms (after all, food goes into the digestive tract which is where the symptoms occur), it is sometimes incorrectly blamed as the trigger for symptoms. In many people, food isn't the main trigger for IBS symptoms but rather psychological factors such as stress, worries, anxiety and depression can be major influences. Some exciting research findings have come about from gut-focused hypnotherapy, cognitive behavioural therapy, mindfulness and other strategies to help these psychological influences. If you feel that these may be impacting on your symptoms, or if you haven't improved after dietary changes, then I recommend speaking with your dietitian. They might recommend a gut-focused clinical hypnotherapist (such as at www.shepherdworks.com.au) or visiting the IBS Clinic website (www.ibsclinic.org.au) or other IBS-focused psychologists who may be able to assist. You should also discuss this with your doctor.

VEGETARIAN EATING ON A LOW-FODMAP DIET

Vegetarian eating may be a religious, lifestyle or other choice, and people who follow a vegetarian diet can indeed eat flavoursome and exciting foods. It's important to ensure that any vegetarian diet provides all the nutrients required daily for good health. A vegetarian meal is not simply a plate of meat and three vegetables with the meat taken off. Such a meal would be lacking in protein, vitamin B12, and other essential nutrients such as iron and zinc.

In a vegetarian diet, legumes (e.g. chickpeas, various dried beans, lentils, lupins and soybeans) are often major sources of protein. While on the Low-FODMAP Diet, particularly in the first step, these foods are restricted. Alternative low-FODMAP vegetarian sources of protein are listed below, and may be sufficiently varied for you in the first step. There are also sample vegetarian and vegan Low-FODMAP Diet menu plans on pages 44–47.

Protein-rich vegetarian foods and beverages:

- *lactose-free milk products (e.g. lactose-free milk and yoghurts) and use the lactase enzyme to enjoy lactose-containing milk-based products (see page 19 or 24)*
- *lactose-free milk-based products such as hard cheeses (see page 26)*
- *eggs*
- *nuts and seeds – except for pistachios and cashews, all other nuts can be enjoyed; nibble in small amounts through the day*
- *nut and/or seed pastes – 1 tablespoon*
- *soy milks made from soybean extract or soy protein (not whole soybeans)*
- *tofu, miso and tempeh, all of which are low-FODMAP even though they're derived from soy*
- *protein-enriched rice, oat or quinoa milks (check ingredients for suitability)*
- *whole grains, e.g. brown rice, buckwheat and quinoa.*

In the second step, you can continue to enjoy the high protein foods listed above and also try to include small amounts of legumes and lentils in your diet (because of their nutritional importance), up to your symptom threshold. Lentils contain fewer FODMAPs than legume beans and chickpeas; ½ cup of cooked, drained lentils contain moderate amounts of GOS and fructans. You might find that you can manage your symptoms by being stricter in cutting out other FODMAP food sources so that you can 'fit' these nutritious foods within your threshold.

Vegetarians should also ensure they have adequate intake of iron and zinc. Good vegetarian sources of iron and zinc include: eggs, quinoa, brown rice, leafy green vegetables and nuts. Iron from plant sources is called non-haem iron, and is not absorbed as well by the body. Try to have a food containing vitamin C with your non-haem-iron foods to optimise iron absorption. Special note for vegans on a Low-FODMAP Diet:

- *It is recommended to consult an Accredited Practising Dietitian if you wish to follow a vegan Low-FODMAP Diet. Without professional advice, it may be difficult to ensure you have an adequate intake of vitamin B12 and protein, and to maintain your energy levels.*
- *Vegans should consult with their doctors to discuss B12 supplements/injections as B12 is only present in animal-derived foods (lacto-ovo vegetarians can get vitamin B12 from eggs and dairy products).*

LOW-FODMAP DIET MENU PLANS

These menu plans will provide you with balanced meals during either one week of the strict phase (Step One) or one week of the reintroduction phase (Step Two). I haven't provided strict quantities because we all have different energy needs and this isn't a weight-loss diet.

STEP ONE LOW-FODMAP MENU PLAN: ADULT

	MONDAY	TUESDAY	WEDNESDAY
BREAKFAST	• Low-FODMAP wholegrain cereal with lactose-free (LF) milk; or gluten-free or low-FODMAP sourdough bread with butter or margarine and jam, peanut butter or Vegemite	• Smoothie made from LF milk, 3 strawberries, ½ banana, 1 teaspoon chia seeds, vanilla extract, cinnamon and ice cubes • Low-FODMAP toast with jam or Vegemite	• Low-FODMAP wholegrain cereal with LF milk; or gluten-free or low-FODMAP sourdough bread with butter or margarine and jam, peanut butter or Vegemite
LUNCH	• Ham and salad sandwich (gluten-free or low-FODMAP sourdough bread, ham, cheese, tomato, alfalfa, lettuce) • 1 serve fruit	• Roast beef and salad sandwich (gluten-free or low-FODMAP sourdough bread, beef, wholegrain mustard, cheese, tomato, lettuce) • 1 serve fruit	• Chicken and Vegetable Soup (page 125) • Gluten-free or low-FODMAP sourdough bread • 1 serve fruit
DINNER	• Seasoned Steak with Spicy Tomato Relish (page 155) • 1 serve chips • Salad made from low-FODMAP vegetables • LF ice cream • 1 serve fruit	• Fettuccine Marinara (page 134) • Salad made from low-FODMAP vegetables • Berry Crumble (page 331)	• Pepper Lamb Stir-fry with Sticky Rice (page 160)

Obviously, the foods listed in Step One menu plans are the low-FODMAP varieties, so 'fruit' will mean balanced fruit and you'll need to check suggested quantities of other foods. See pages 26–27 for a list of suitable foods and also refer to Low-FODMAP Shopping Guide 6th edition for suitable commercial packaged foods, available from www.shepherdworks.com.au.

Note that the following low-FODMAP menu plans have some gluten-containing suggestions. Please choose only gluten-free foods if you also follow a gluten-free diet. When a meal calls for sandwich bread, use a maximum of two slices in the meal. Also note LF means lactose-free (not low-fat).

THURSDAY	FRIDAY	SATURDAY	SUNDAY
• Low-FODMAP wholegrain cereal with LF milk; or gluten-free or low-FODMAP sourdough bread with butter or margarine and jam, peanut butter or Vegemite	• Smoothie made from LF milk, 3 strawberries, 10 blueberries, 5 raspberries, 1 teaspoon chia seeds, maple syrup and ice cubes • Low-FODMAP toast with jam or Vegemite	• Low-FODMAP wholegrain cereal with LF milk; or gluten-free or low-FODMAP sourdough bread with butter or margarine and jam, peanut butter or Vegemite	• Spanish Omelette (page 107) • Gluten-free or low-FODMAP sourdough bread with butter or margarine
• Chicken and Quinoa Salad (page 118) • 1 serve fruit	• Egg and salad sandwich (gluten-free or low-FODMAP sourdough bread, boiled egg, tomato, cucumber, lettuce, 1 teaspoon mayonnaise) • 1 serve fruit	• Toasted ham and cheese sandwich (gluten-free or low-FODMAP sourdough bread, ham, cheese, tomato) • 1 serve fruit	• Individual Caesar Salads with Garlic-flavoured Croutons (page 114) • 1 LF yoghurt • 1 serve fruit
• Trevally with Lemongrass Chilli Noodles (page 149) • Buckwheat noodles • LF ice cream	• Marinated Pork Ribs with Creamy Mash (page 164) • Lemon Soufflé (page 226)	• Chicken Parmigiana (page 174) • Salad made from low-FODMAP vegetables	• Roast Beef with Fragrant Asian Flavours (page 154) • Roast potato and green vegetables • Lime Tart (page 230)

STEP ONE LOW-FODMAP MENU PLAN: KIDS

	MONDAY	TUESDAY	WEDNESDAY
BREAKFAST	• Low-FODMAP wholegrain cereal with lactose-free (LF) milk; or gluten-free or low-FODMAP sourdough bread with butter or margarine and jam, peanut butter or Vegemite	• Smoothie made from LF milk, 3 strawberries, ½ banana, 1 teaspoon chia seeds, vanilla extract, cinnamon and ice cubes • Low-FODMAP toast with jam or Vegemite	• Low-FODMAP wholegrain cereal with LF milk; or gluten-free or low-FODMAP sourdough bread with butter or margarine and jam, peanut butter or Vegemite
LUNCH	• Omelette Wraps (page 206) • 1 serve fruit	• Ham and salad sandwich (gluten-free or low-FODMAP sourdough bread, beef, cheese, tomato, lettuce) • 1 serve fruit	• Omelette Wraps (page 206) • 1 serve fruit
DINNER	• Chicken Fried Rice (page 209) • LF ice cream • 1 serve fruit	• Meatballs with Pasta (page 200) • Salad made from low-FODMAP vegetables • Berry Crumble (page 221)	• Beef and Vegetable Skewers (page 210) • Gingerbread Ice-Cream Cookies (page 242)

THURSDAY	FRIDAY	SATURDAY	SUNDAY
• Low-FODMAP wholegrain cereal with LF milk; or gluten-free or low-FODMAP sourdough bread with butter or margarine and jam, peanut butter or Vegemite	• Smoothie made from LF milk, 3 strawberries, 10 blueberries, 5 raspberries, 1 teaspoon chia seeds, maple syrup and ice cubes • Low-FODMAP toast with jam or Vegemite	• Low-FODMAP wholegrain cereal with LF milk; or gluten-free or low-FODMAP sourdough bread with butter or margarine and jam, peanut butter or Vegemite	• Buttermilk Pancakes with Blueberry Compote (page 104)
• Chicken Drumsticks (page 203) • 1 serve fruit	• Chicken and salad sandwich (gluten-free or low-FODMAP sourdough bread, chicken, tomato, cucumber, lettuce, 1 teaspoon mayonnaise) • 1 serve fruit	• Toasted ham and cheese sandwich (gluten-free or low-FODMAP sourdough bread, ham, cheese) • Carrot, cucumber and capsicum sticks • 1 serve fruit	• Mini Quiches (page 214) • 1 LF yoghurt • 1 serve fruit
• Fish in Batter (page 204) • 1 serve chips • Salad made from low-FODMAP vegetables	• Meatloaf (page 207) • 1 serve chips • Salad made from low-FODMAP vegetables • Lemon Soufflé (page 226)	• Chicken Parmigiana (page 174) • Salad made from low-FODMAP vegetables	• Lasagne (page 213) • Mashed potato and green vegetables • Chocolate Puddings (page 218)

STEP ONE LOW-FODMAP MENU PLAN: LACTO-OVO VEGETARIAN ADULT

	MONDAY	TUESDAY	WEDNESDAY
BREAKFAST	• Low-FODMAP wholegrain cereal with lactose-free (LF) lite milk; or gluten-free or low-FODMAP sourdough bread with butter or margarine and jam, peanut butter or Vegemite	• Gluten-free or low-FODMAP sourdough bread with butter or margarine and jam, peanut butter or Vegemite	• Low-FODMAP wholegrain cereal with LF lite milk; or gluten-free or low-FODMAP sourdough bread with butter or margarine and jam, peanut butter or Vegemite
LUNCH	• Cheese and salad sandwich (gluten-free or low-FODMAP sourdough bread, cheese, tomato, lettuce) • 1 serve fruit	• Egg and salad sandwich (gluten-free or low-FODMAP sourdough bread, boiled egg, tomato, cheese, lettuce) • 1 serve fruit	• Roasted Pumpkin and Ginger Soup (page 126) • Gluten-free or low-FODMAP sourdough bread • 1 serve fruit
DINNER	• Quinoa with Capsicum, Basil and Lemon (page 196) • LF ice cream • 1 serve fruit	• Four Cheese Risotto (page 184) • Salad made from low-FODMAP vegetables • Berry Crumble (page 221)	• Stir-fried Soba Noodles (page 191)

THURSDAY	FRIDAY	SATURDAY	SUNDAY
• Low-FODMAP wholegrain cereal with LF lite milk; or gluten-free or low-FODMAP sourdough bread with butter or margarine and jam, peanut butter or Vegemite	• Smoothie made from LF lite milk, 3 strawberries, 10 blueberries, 5 raspberries, 1 teaspoon chia seeds, maple syrup and ice cubes • Gluten-free or low-FODMAP sourdough bread with butter or margarine and jam, peanut butter or Vegemite	• Low-FODMAP wholegrain cereal with LF lite milk; or gluten-free or low-FODMAP sourdough bread with butter or margarine and jam, peanut butter or Vegemite	• Asian Omelette (page 190) • Gluten-free or low-FODMAP sourdough bread with butter or margarine
• Moroccan Roast Vegetable Salad (page 117) • 1 serve fruit	• Egg and salad sandwich (gluten-free or low-FODMAP sourdough bread, boiled egg, tomato, cucumber, lettuce, 1 teaspoon mayonnaise) • 1 serve fruit	• Toasted tomato and cheese sandwich (gluten-free or low-FODMAP sourdough bread, tomato, cheese) • Side salad made from low-FODMAP vegetables • 1 serve fruit	• Pumpkin, Pecan and Blue Cheese Salad (page 113) • 1 LF yoghurt • 1 serve fruit
• Pan-fried Gnocchi with Roasted Capsicum Sauce (page 188) • LF ice cream	• Goat's Cheese and Sweet Potato Frittata (page 192) • Salad made from low-FODMAP vegetables • Lemon Soufflé (page 226)	• Pasta Puttanesca (page 195) • Salad made from low-FODMAP vegetables	• Tomato, Basil and Mozzarella Arancini (page 186) • Carrot, green vegetables • Lime Tart (page 230)

STEP ONE LOW-FODMAP MENU PLAN: VEGAN ADULT

	MONDAY	TUESDAY	WEDNESDAY
BREAKFAST	• Quinoa cooked in coconut milk served with blueberries and maple syrup	• Low-FODMAP wholegrain cereal with rice or oat milk; or gluten-free or low-FODMAP sourdough bread with dairy-free spread and jam, peanut butter or Vegemite	• Vegan smoothie made from rice or oat milk, ½ avocado, ½ banana, 1 tablespoon pepitas, vanilla extract and ice cubes
LUNCH	• Vegan meat-free slice* and salad sandwich (gluten-free or low-FODMAP sourdough bread vegan slice, tomato, lettuce, alfalfa, 1–2 teaspoon tahini) • 1 serve fruit and small handful of low-FODMAP nuts and/or seeds	• Vegan cheese and salad sandwich (gluten-free or low-FODMAP sourdough bread, low-FODMAP vegan cheese, tomato, lettuce, cucumber, carrot) • 1 serve fruit and small handful of low-FODMAP nuts and/or seeds	• Roasted Pumpkin and Ginger Soup (page 126) • Gluten-free or low-FODMAP sourdough bread • 1 serve fruit and small handful of low-FODMAP nuts and/or seeds
DINNER	• Quinoa with Capsicum, Basil and Lemon (page 196) – replace feta with low-FODMAP vegan cheese • 1 serve fruit	• Pepper Tofu Stir-fry with Sticky Rice (page 160) – replace lamb with tofu and remove oyster sauce	• Stir-fried Soba Noodles (page 191)

THURSDAY	FRIDAY	SATURDAY	SUNDAY
• Gluten-free or low-FODMAP sourdough bread with dairy-free spread, peanut butter and sliced banana • Glass of rice or oat milk	• Gluten-free or low-FODMAP sourdough bread with vegan cream cheese and sliced strawberries • Glass of rice or oat milk	• Vegan smoothie made from rice or oat milk, 3 strawberries, ½ banana, 1 tablespoon rice protein powder, 1 teaspoon chia seeds, vanilla extract and ice cubes	• Vanilla 'Porridge' with Strawberry and Rhubarb Compote and Granola (page 99) – substitute milk with oat or rice milk
• Moroccan Roast Vegetable Salad (page 117) – served with ½ cup cooked drained lentils • 1 serve fruit and small handful of low-FODMAP nuts and/ or seeds	• Vegan meat-free slice* and salad sandwich (gluten-free or low-FODMAP sourdough bread, vegan slice, tomato, cucumber, lettuce, avocado, egg- and dairy-free mayonnaise) • 1 serve fruit and small handful of low-FODMAP nuts and/ or seeds	• Schnitzel* and salad sandwich (gluten-free or low-FODMAP sourdough bread, cooked vegan crumbed schnitzel, tomato, lettuce) • 1 serve fruit and small handful of low-FODMAP nuts and/ or seeds	• Vegetable Soup (page 125) – replace all chicken with 1 cup of cooked drained lentils, use onion-free vegetable stock • 1 serve fruit and small handful of low-FODMAP nuts and/ or seeds
• Wheat-free Pasta with Roasted Capsicum Sauce using recipe from Pan-fried Gnocchi (page 188)	• Tofu and Vegetable Skewers (page 210) – replace beef with tofu	• Pasta Puttanesca (page 195) • Lettuce, cucumber, tomato	• Tofu Fried Rice (page 209) – replace chicken with tofu, use brown rice instead of white • Sweet potato, green vegetables

* Available from vegetarian-refrigerated deli or freezer sections of supermarket, check ingredients to ensure low-FODMAP.

STEP TWO LOW-FODMAP MENU PLAN WITH LACTOSE: ADULT

	MONDAY	TUESDAY	WEDNESDAY
BREAKFAST	• Gluten-free or low-FODMAP sourdough bread with butter or margarine and jam, peanut butter or Vegemite	• Smoothie made from lite milk, 3 strawberries, ½ banana, 1 teaspoon chia seeds, vanilla extract, cinnamon and ice cubes	• Gluten-free or low-FODMAP sourdough bread with butter or margarine and jam, peanut butter or Vegemite
LUNCH	• Ham and salad sandwich (gluten-free or low-FODMAP sourdough bread, ham, cheese, tomato, lettuce) • 1 serve fruit	• Beef and salad sandwich (gluten-free or low-FODMAP sourdough bread, beef, cheese, tomato, lettuce) • 1 serve fruit	• Chicken and Vegetable Soup (page 125) • Yoghurt • 1 serve fruit
DINNER	• Beef Bourguignon with Parsnip Croquettes (page 156) • Orange vegetable, green vegetable • 1 serve fruit	• Saffron Chicken Pasta with Summer Vegetables (page 138) • Basil-infused Panna Cotta (page 233)	• Lasagne (page 213) • Green vegetable, orange vegetable

THURSDAY	FRIDAY	SATURDAY	SUNDAY
• Gluten-free or low-FODMAP sourdough bread with butter or margarine and jam, peanut butter or Vegemite	• Smoothie made from lite milk, 3 strawberries, 10 blueberries, 5 raspberries, 1 teaspoon chia seeds, maple syrup and ice cubes	• Gluten-free or low-FODMAP sourdough bread with butter or margarine and jam, peanut butter or Vegemite	• Vanilla 'Porridge' with Strawberry and Rhubarb Compote and Granola (page 99)
• Moroccan Roast Vegetable Salad (page 117) • 1 serve fruit	• Egg and salad sandwich (gluten-free or low-FODMAP sourdough bread, boiled egg, tomato, cucumber, lettuce, 1 teaspoon mayonnaise) • 1 serve fruit	• Toasted ham and cheese sandwich (gluten-free or low-FODMAP sourdough bread, ham, cheese) • Tomato, lettuce, cottage cheese • 1 serve fruit	• Pumpkin, Pecan and Blue Cheese Salad (page 113) • 1 low-fat yoghurt • 1 serve fruit
• Thai-style Salmon with Coconut Rice (page 150)	• Crisp-skin Pork Belly with Spiced Pumpkin (page 168) • Low-FODMAP vegetables	• Chicken Tagine (page 178) • Lemon Coconut Cheesecake (page 241)	• Roast Lamb with Rosemary Potatoes (page 163) • Carrots, green vegetables • Salted Caramel Custard Puddings (page 225)

STEP TWO LOW-FODMAP MENU PLAN WITH MANNITOL: ADULT

	MONDAY	TUESDAY	WEDNESDAY
BREAKFAST	• Low-FODMAP wholegrain cereal with lactose-free (LF) milk; or gluten-free or low-FODMAP sourdough bread with butter or margarine and jam, peanut butter or Vegemite	• Smoothie made from LF milk, 3 strawberries, ½ banana, 1 teaspoon chia seeds, vanilla extract, cinnamon and ice cubes	• Low-FODMAP wholegrain cereal with LF milk; or gluten-free or low-FODMAP sourdough bread with butter or margarine and jam, peanut butter or Vegemite
LUNCH	• Ham and salad sandwich (gluten-free or low-FODMAP sourdough bread, ham, cheese, tomato, lettuce) • 1 serve fruit	• Beef and salad sandwich (gluten-free or low-FODMAP sourdough bread, beef, cheese, tomato, lettuce) • 1 serve fruit	• Omelette Wraps (page 206) • 1 serve fruit
DINNER	• Pepper Lamb Stir-fry with Sticky Rice (page 160) – add mushrooms • LF ice cream • 1 serve fruit	• Saffron Chicken Pasta with Summer Vegetables (page 138) • Basil-infused Panna Cotta (page 233)	• Pan-fried Gnocchi with Roasted Capsicum Sauce (page 188)

THURSDAY	FRIDAY	SATURDAY	SUNDAY
• Low-FODMAP wholegrain cereal with LF milk; or gluten-free or low-FODMAP sourdough bread with butter or margarine and jam, peanut butter or Vegemite	• Smoothie made from LF milk, 3 strawberries, 10 blueberries, 5 raspberries, 1 teaspoon chia seeds, maple syrup and ice cubes	• Low-FODMAP wholegrain cereal with LF milk; or gluten-free or low-FODMAP sourdough bread with butter or margarine and jam, peanut butter or Vegemite	• Asian Omelette (page 190)
• Moroccan Roast Vegetable Salad (page 117) • 1 serve fruit	• Egg and salad sandwich (gluten-free or low-FODMAP sourdough bread, boiled egg, tomato, cucumber, lettuce, 1 teaspoon mayonnaise) • 1 serve fruit	• Toasted ham and cheese sandwich (gluten-free or low-FODMAP sourdough bread, ham, cheese) • Low-FODMAP side salad • 1 serve fruit	• Chicken and Vegetable Soup with Cauliflower (page 125) • 1 LF yoghurt • 1 serve fruit
• Thai-style Salmon with Coconut Rice (page 150)	• Beef Noodle Soup (page 122) – add mushrooms to broth	• Chicken Tagine (page 178) • Chocolate Puddings (page 218)	• Beef Bourguignon with Parsnip Croquettes (page 156) • Orange vegetable, green vegetable • Passionfruit Brûlée (page 222)

STEP TWO LOW-FODMAP MENU PLAN WITH SORBITOL: ADULT

	MONDAY	TUESDAY	WEDNESDAY
BREAKFAST	• Low-FODMAP wholegrain cereal with lactose-free (LF) milk; or gluten-free or low-FODMAP sourdough bread with butter or margarine, and jam, peanut butter or Vegemite	• Smoothie made from LF milk, 3 strawberries, ½ banana, 1 teaspoon chia seeds, vanilla extract, cinnamon and ice cubes	• Wheat-free cereal with LF milk; or gluten-free or low-FODMAP sourdough bread with butter or margarine, and jam, peanut butter or Vegemite
LUNCH	• Ham and salad sandwich (gluten-free or low-FODMAP sourdough bread, ham, cheese, tomato, lettuce) • 1 serve fruit	• Beef and salad sandwich (gluten-free or low-FODMAP sourdough bread, beef, cheese, tomato, lettuce) • 4 dried apricot halves	• Omelette Wraps (page 206) • 1 serve fruit
DINNER	• Pepper Lamb Stir-fry with Sticky Rice (page 160) • LF ice cream • 1 serve fruit	• Saffron Chicken Pasta with Summer Vegetables (page 138) • Berry Crumble (page 221)	• Lasagne (page 213) • Orange vegetable, green vegetable, potato

THURSDAY	FRIDAY	SATURDAY	SUNDAY
• Low-FODMAP wholegrain cereal with LF milk; or gluten-free or low-FODMAP sourdough bread with butter or margarine, and jam, peanut butter or Vegemite	• Smoothie made from LF milk, 2 apricots, 1 teaspoon chia seeds, maple syrup and ice cubes	• Low-FODMAP wholegrain cereal with LF milk; or gluten-free or low-FODMAP sourdough bread with butter or margarine, and jam, peanut butter or Vegemite	• Corn Fritters with Herbed Ricotta, Avocado and Tomatoes (page 100)
• Moroccan Roast Vegetable Salad (page 117) • 1 serve fruit	• Egg and salad sandwich (gluten-free or low-FODMAP sourdough bread, boiled egg, tomato, cucumber, lettuce, 1 teaspoon mayonnaise) • 1 serve fruit	• Toasted ham and cheese sandwich (gluten-free or low-FODMAP sourdough bread, ham, cheese) • Side salad with Low-FODMAP vegetables • 1 serve fruit	• Chicken and Vegetable Soup (page 125) • 1 LF yoghurt • 1 serve fruit
• Thai-style Salmon with Coconut Rice (page 150)	• Crisp-skin Pork Belly with Spiced Pumpkin (page 168) • Low-FODMAP vegetables	• Chicken Tagine (page 178) • Salted Caramel Custard Puddings (page 225)	• Beef Bourguignon with Parsnip Croquettes (page 156) • Orange vegetable, green vegetable • Blackberry and Hazelnut Cake (page 224) – use blackberries instead of strawberries

STEP TWO LOW-FODMAP MENU PLAN WITH EXCESS FRUCTOSE: ADULT

	MONDAY	TUESDAY	WEDNESDAY
BREAKFAST	• Low-FODMAP wholegrain cereal with low fat (LF) milk; or gluten-free or low-FODMAP sourdough bread with butter or margarine and honey	• Smoothie made from LF milk, 1 mango cheek, ½ banana, 1 teaspoon chia seeds, vanilla extract and ice cubes	• Low-FODMAP wholegrain cereal with LF milk; or gluten-free or low-FODMAP sourdough bread with butter, margarine or peanut butter
LUNCH	• Ham and salad sandwich (gluten-free or low-FODMAP sourdough bread, ham, cheese, tomato, lettuce) • 1 serve fruit	• Beef and salad sandwich (gluten-free or low-FODMAP sourdough bread, beef, cheese, tomato, lettuce) • 1 serve fruit	• Omelette Wraps (page 206) • 1 serve fruit
DINNER	• Pepper Lamb Stir-fry with Sticky Rice (page 160) – add sugar-snap peas • LF ice cream	• Saffron Chicken Pasta with Summer Vegetables (page 138) • Berry Crumble (page 221)	• Lasagne (page 213) • Orange vegetable, green vegetable, potato

THURSDAY	FRIDAY	SATURDAY	SUNDAY
• Low-FODMAP wholegrain cereal with LF milk; or gluten-free or low-FODMAP sourdough bread with butter or margarine and honey	• Smoothie made from LF milk, 3 strawberries, 10 blueberries, 5 raspberries, 1 teaspoon chia seeds and ice cubes	• Low-FODMAP wholegrain cereal with LF milk; or gluten-free or low-FODMAP sourdough bread with butter or margarine and honey	• Buttermilk Pancakes with Blueberry Compote (page 104)
• Moroccan Roast Vegetable Salad (page 117) • 1 serve fruit	• Egg and salad sandwich (gluten-free or low-FODMAP sourdough bread, boiled egg, tomato, cucumber, lettuce, 1 teaspoon mayonnaise) • 1 serve fruit	• Toasted ham and cheese sandwich (gluten-free or low-FODMAP sourdough bread, ham, cheese) • Side salad with low-FODMAP vegetables • 1 serve fruit	• Chicken and Vegetable Soup (page 125) • 1 LF yoghurt • 1 serve fruit
• Thai-style Salmon with Coconut Rice (page 150)	• Crisp-skin Pork Belly with Spiced Pumpkin (page 168) • Low-FODMAP vegetables	• Chicken Tagine (page 178) • Salted Caramel Custard Puddings (page 225)	• Beef Bourguignon with Parsnip Croquettes (page 156) • Orange vegetable, green vegetable • Strawberry and Hazelnut Cake (page 224)

STEP TWO LOW-FODMAP MENU PLAN WITH FRUCTANS: ADULT

	MONDAY	TUESDAY	WEDNESDAY
BREAKFAST	• Wheat bread with butter or margarine and jam, peanut butter or Vegemite	• Smoothie made from lactose-free (LF) milk, 3 strawberries, ½ banana, 1 teaspoon chia seeds, vanilla extract, cinnamon and ice cubes	• Low-FODMAP wholegrain cereal with LF milk; or gluten-free or low-FODMAP sourdough bread with butter or margarine and jam, peanut butter or Vegemite
LUNCH	• Ham and salad sandwich (gluten-free or low-FODMAP sourdough bread, ham, cheese, tomato, lettuce) • 1 serve fruit	• Beef and salad sandwich (gluten-free or low-FODMAP sourdough bread, beef, tomato, cheese, lettuce) • 1 serve fruit	• Roasted Pumpkin and Ginger Soup (page 126) • Wheat-based bread • 1 serve fruit
DINNER	• Beef Bourguignon with Parsnip Croquettes (page 156) • Orange vegetable, green vegetable • 1 serve fruit	• Saffron Chicken Pasta with Summer Vegetables (page 138)	• Lasagne (page 213) • Green vegetable, orange vegetable

THURSDAY	FRIDAY	SATURDAY	SUNDAY
• Low-FODMAP wholegrain cereal with LF milk; or gluten-free or low-FODMAP sourdough bread with butter or margarine and jam, peanut butter or Vegemite	• Smoothie made from LF milk, 3 strawberries, 10 blueberries, 5 raspberries, 1 teaspoon chia seeds, maple syrup and ice cubes	• Quinoa cooked in coconut milk served with blueberries and maple syrup	• Corn Fritters with Herbed Ricotta, Avocado and Tomatoes (page 100) – use wheat flour
• Moroccan Roast Vegetable Salad (page 117) – using garlic • 1 serve fruit	• Egg and salad sandwich (wheat bread, boiled egg, tomato, cucumber, lettuce, 1 teaspoon mayonnaise) • 1 serve fruit	• Toasted ham and cheese sandwich (gluten-free or low-FODMAP sourdough bread, ham, cheese) • Side salad with low-FODMAP vegetables • 1 serve fruit	• Pumpkin, Pecan and Blue Cheese Salad (page 113) • LF yoghurt • 1 serve fruit
• Thai-style Salmon with Coconut Rice (page 150)	• Crisp-skin Pork Belly with Spiced Pumpkin (page 168) • Low -FODMAP vegetables	• Chicken Tagine (page 178) • Chocolate Puddings (page 218)	• Roast Lamb with Rosemary Potatoes (page 163) • Carrots, green vegetables • Passionfruit Brûlée (page 222)

STEP TWO LOW-FODMAP MENU PLAN GOS (AND SOME FRUCTAN TOLERANCE): ADULT

	MONDAY	TUESDAY	WEDNESDAY
BREAKFAST	• Low-FODMAP wholegrain cereal with lactose-free (LF) milk; or gluten-free or low-FODMAP sourdough bread with butter or margarine and jam, peanut butter or Vegemite	• Smoothie made from LF milk, 3 strawberries, ½ banana, 1 teaspoon chia seeds, vanilla extract, cinnamon and ice cubes	• Low-FODMAP wholegrain cereal with LF milk; or gluten-free or low-FODMAP sourdough bread with butter or margarine and jam, peanut butter or Vegemite
LUNCH	• Ham and salad sandwich (gluten-free or low-FODMAP sourdough bread, ham, cheese, tomato, lettuce) • 1 serve fruit	• Beef and salad sandwich (gluten-free or low-FODMAP sourdough bread, beef, tomato, cheese, lettuce) • 1 serve fruit	• Chicken and Vegetable Soup (page 125) – made with ½ cup cooked drained lentils • Gluten-free or low-FODMAP sourdough bread • 1 serve fruit
DINNER	• Beef Bourguignon with Parsnip Croquettes (page 156) • Orange vegetable, green vegetable • 1 serve fruit	• Saffron Chicken Pasta with Summer Vegetables (page 138)	• Lasagne (page 213) • Low-FODMAP vegetables

THURSDAY	FRIDAY	SATURDAY	SUNDAY
• Low-FODMAP wholegrain cereal with LF milk; or gluten-free or low-FODMAP sourdough bread with butter or margarine and jam, peanut butter or Vegemite	• Smoothie made from LF milk, 3 strawberries, 10 blueberries, 5 raspberries, 1 teaspoon chia seeds, maple syrup, ice cubes	• Quinoa cooked in coconut milk served with blueberries and maple syrup	• Scrambled Eggs on Cornbread (page 96) – with ½ cup baked beans
• Moroccan Roast Vegetable Salad (page 117) – served with ½ cup cooked drained chickpeas • 1 serve fruit	• Egg and salad sandwich (gluten-free or low-FODMAP sourdough bread, boiled egg, tomato, cucumber, lettuce, 1 teaspoon mayonnaise) • 1 serve fruit	• Toasted ham and cheese sandwich (gluten-free or low-FODMAP sourdough bread, ham, cheese) • Side salad with low-FODMAP vegetables • 1 serve fruit	• Pumpkin, Pecan and Blue Cheese Salad (page 113) • LF yoghurt • 1 serve fruit
• Thai-style Salmon with Coconut Rice (page 150)	• Crisp-skin Pork Belly with Spiced Pumpkin (page 168) • Low-FODMAP vegetables	• Chicken Tagine (page 178) • Chocolate Puddings (page 218)	• Roast Lamb with Rosemary Potatoes (page 163) • Low-FODMAP vegetables • Passionfruit Brûlée (page 222)

4. SHOPPING FOR A LOW-FODMAP DIET

SHOPPING FOR LOW-FODMAP FOODS

Low-FODMAP Diet Food Shopping Guide

I have produced a very handy shopping guide that can fit in your back pocket or handbag when you go shopping for your Low-FODMAP Diet. It details an enormous number of foods available in Australia that have low-FODMAP ingredients. The *Low-FODMAP Diet Food Shopping Guide* also has useful background information, explanatory notes, and foods are coded so people can tailor their food choices according to their own individual FODMAP tolerance! For the convenience of many, gluten has also been identified even though gluten is not a FODMAP.

Bursting with over 190 pages of information about hundreds of products and with lots of photographs throughout, this is sure to help you and your tummy be more than satisfied. Available from www.shepherdworks.com.au

FINDING FODMAP-FRIENDLY FOODS

The 'FODMAP Friendly' certification program, incorporating the 'FODMAP Friendly' logo is designed to help people shopping for a Low-FODMAP Diet identify and select suitable food products. All products showing the logo have been tested and laboratory-proven to have 'FODMAP Friendly' minimal levels of fructose, fructans, galacto-oligosaccharides, sorbitol, mannitol and lactose per serve. It's much more convenient than reading food product labels and it helps you select suitable foods without requiring an in-depth understanding of the interactions between different ingredients or overall FODMAP levels.

USING FOOD LABELS

When reading food labels, it's important to bear in mind that even when the ingredients list on a label includes ingredients identified in this book as being high in FODMAPs, the whole food itself may not be high-FODMAP.

On food labels, the ingredients are listed in descending order by weight. This means that the ingredients listed first are present in the greatest amounts, and the ingredients listed last are in the smallest amounts. As a general rule, if a high-FODMAP food – for example, onion, garlic or honey – is one of the very last ingredients, or is indicated on the label to make up less than 5 per cent of the total product, it's likely that, overall, the complete food will be low-FODMAP. See the label-reading examples on page 63 for more help with interpreting food labels.

It's important to note that people on a Low-FODMAP Diet need not avoid every wheat ingredient – many are safe ...

Food labelling for wheat

Food-labelling laws in Australia make it compulsory for food manufacturers to declare all wheat-derived ingredients on the food label. It's important to note that people on a Low-FODMAP Diet need not avoid every wheat ingredient – many are safe, as they are chains of glucose molecules and don't contain fructans. Examples include:

- wheat starch or wheat thickeners, which are chains of many (even hundreds of) glucose molecules joined together
- wheat maltodextrin or wheat dextrin, which are shorter chains of glucose molecules joined together
- wheat dextrose, which is a chain of two or three glucose molecules
- wheat glucose, which is a single glucose molecule
- wheat colour caramel (made as a derivative of glucose syrup).

LOW-WHEAT VERSUS GLUTEN-FREE

A Low-FODMAP Diet is not a gluten-free diet! People following a Low-FODMAP Diet don't need a gluten-free diet but can enjoy many gluten-free foods (unless they contain another type of FODMAP). For more information, see page 267.

Food additives

A number of food additives are permitted for use in processed foods. People on a Low-FODMAP Diet should *restrict* these food additives, which are sweeteners and humectants:

- sorbitol (420)
- mannitol (421)
- xylitol (967)
- maltitol (965)
- isomalt — contains sorbitol and mannitol (953)
- polydextrose — 10 per cent sorbitol (1200).

These food additives, however, are *low-FODMAP*:

- acidity regulators
- anti-caking agents
- antifoaming agents
- antioxidants
- bulking agents
- colour fixatives
- colourings
- emulsifiers
- enzymes
- firming agents
- flavour enhancers
- flavours
- foaming agents
- gelling agents
- glazing agents
- mineral salts
- preservatives
- propellants
- raising agents
- sequestrants
- stabilisers
- sweeteners (other than those listed above)
- thickeners.

Even if the thickeners or other food additives are declared on the label as being made from wheat, they are suitable on a Low-FODMAP Diet as the amount and type of wheat present is not a problem, as described on page 61.

HOW TO INTERPRET FOOD LABELS

Example 1: Satay Stir-fry Sauce

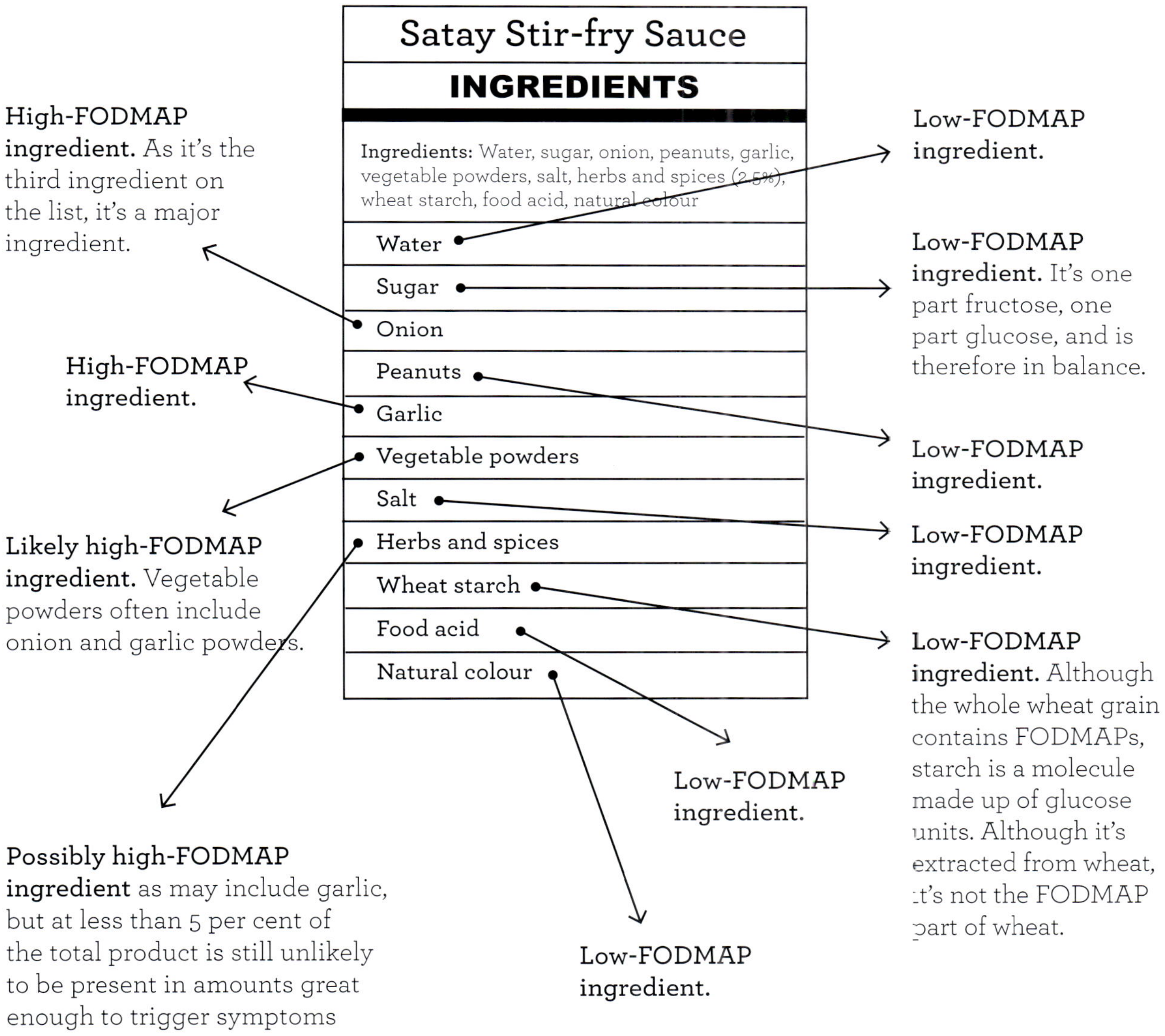

Verdict: high FODMAP, not suitable

Example 2: Liquid Chicken Gravy

Liquid Chicken Gravy

INGREDIENTS

Ingredients: Water, thickener 1442, skim milk powder, salt, corn starch, wheat flour, sugar, yeast extract, onion powder (2%), chicken powder, barley extract (gluten), natural colour

- Water — **Low-FODMAP ingredient.**
- Thickener 1442 — **Low-FODMAP ingredient.** As explained on page 62, thickeners are low-FODMAP food additives. Sometimes thickeners are made from wheat, but they contain only molecules made up of glucose units and so don't include the FODMAP part of wheat.
- Skim milk powder — **Low-FODMAP ingredient.** Although skim milk powder can be a source of lactose, the amount in this gravy is less than the amount of thickener present so it will be there in a small amount. The portion of gravy served with a meal would be small, so the amount of lactose in a serve would be minimal. Even people who are lactose-intolerant can tolerate 4 grams of lactose in a sitting, and the amount of lactose in this gravy would be estimated to be under this threshold.
- Salt — **Low-FODMAP ingredient.**
- Corn starch — **Low-FODMAP ingredient.**
- Wheat flour — **Low-FODMAP ingredient.** Although the whole wheat grain contains FODMAPs, and flour is made from the whole wheat grain, the amount of FODMAP present is so low, it wouldn't contribute a problem amount to the whole gravy sauce, especially in such a small serve.
- Sugar — **Low-FODMAP ingredient.** It's one part fructose, one part glucose, and is therefore in balance.
- Yeast extract — **Low-FODMAP ingredient.**
- Onion powder — **Potentially high-FODMAP ingredient,** but as it's used in very small amounts – less than 5 per cent of the final product, it's unlikely to contribute a problem amount of FODMAPs to the whole gravy.
- Chicken powder — **Low-FODMAP ingredient.**
- Barley extract (gluten) — **Low-FODMAP ingredient.** Gluten is not a problem on a Low-FODMAP Diet.
- Natural colour — **Low-FODMAP ingredient.**

Verdict: low FODMAP, suitable

Example 3: Fruit-free Muesli

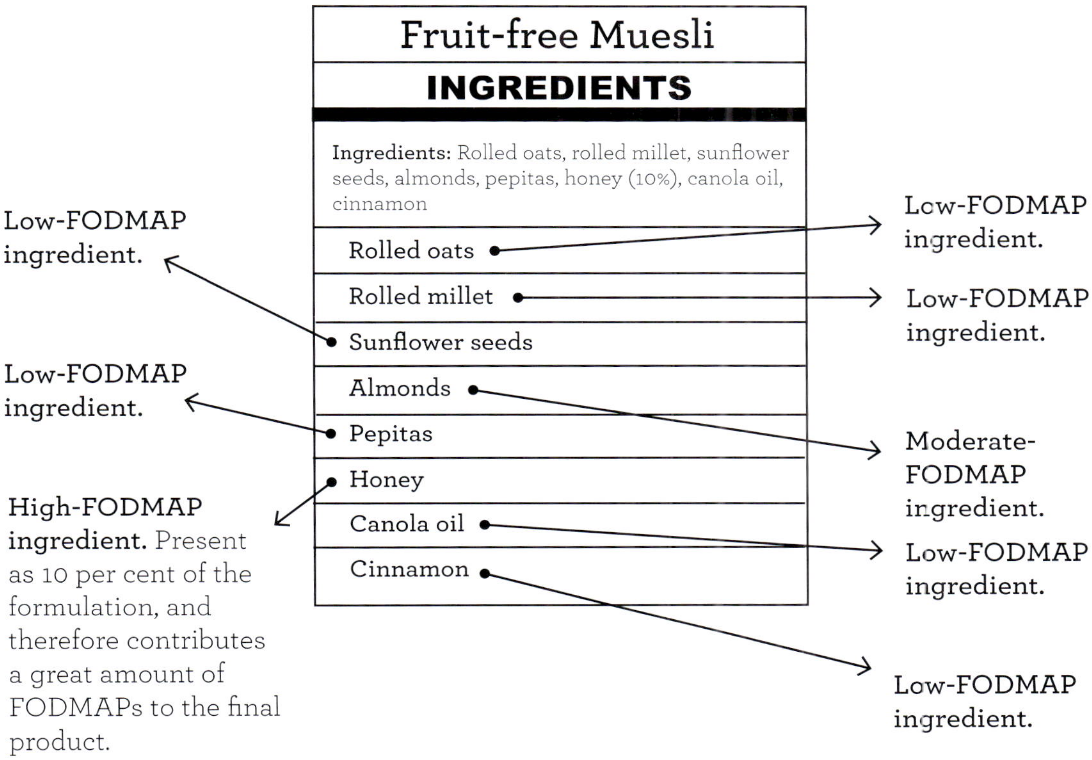

Verdict: high FODMAP, not suitable

STOCKING THE PANTRY

For fabulous low-FODMAP meals, I recommend equipping your kitchen with the useful staple ingredients listed on page 66. You'll notice in the recipes that I use a combination of flours. Some flours in the list appear as 'highly recommended' because these, together with xanthan gum, will help create delicious baked goodies. No single flour substitutes directly for wheat flour so I recommend using a combination of flours to make a 'wheat equivalent' flour blend. Different blends are used for different purposes – while one combination of flours will work for cakes, a different combination will work well for biscuits or pastry. The list highlights these flours, sauces, oils and other important ingredients for your kitchen.

INGREDIENT TYPE	INGREDIENT
Flours *Highly recommended*	■ Cornflour – made from maize (corn) ■ Potato flour ■ Rice flour – fine ■ Soy flour* ■ Tapioca flour
Flours *Recommended*	■ Arrowroot ■ Brown rice flour ■ Buckwheat flour – some are blends and may contain wheat flour ■ Chickpea/besan flour* – can be used as an alternative to soy ■ Millet flour ■ Sorghum flour ■ Quinoa flour
Oils	■ Cooking oil (e.g. canola oil) ■ Olive oil – garlic-infused, lemon-infused, onion-infused
Sauces and dressings	■ Fish sauce ■ Garlic-free – oyster sauce, salad dressing, sweet chilli sauce, tomato sauce ■ Mayonnaise ■ Onion-free salad dressing ■ Soy sauce
Other	■ Almond meal* ■ Balsamic vinegar ■ Cocoa ■ Herbs and spices (see page 91) ■ Hazelnut meal ■ Polenta ■ Vanilla essence ■ Wheat-free breadcrumbs ■ Xanthan gum

* These contain galacto-oligosaccharides and fructans, but as the amount used in a whole recipe is only small, the amount present in a serving size has been found not to cause IBS symptoms in most people. Assess your individual tolerance.

“I’m 22 years old. I have suffered from horrible IBS symptoms my entire life, and over my entire life I’ve been through many tests for coeliac disease, lactose and fructose intolerance. Up until Christmas Day, nobody had been able to tell me anything or help me manage my symptoms. My cousin showed me your Low-FODMAP diet in your book, The Food Intolerance Management Plan, and it has been a godsend to me. I want to thank you for your work. I’ve suffered badly from my IBS and now I can live normally and enjoy life more.”

5. THE LOW-FODMAP DIET FOR CHILDREN

The Low-FODMAP Diet can work well to relieve IBS symptoms in children, just as it does in adults. Children do not always eat under your supervision – such as at friends' parties, sleepovers and school camps. This chapter provides child-specific tips for implementing the Low-FODMAP Diet to help guide you through these experiences with your child. An important point to note is that, to our knowledge, although at worst FODMAPs trigger IBS symptoms, they cause no physical damage to the bowels. This means that if your child eats FODMAPs when they're away from you, it should not cause any lasting damage.

It's important to work with your child's needs. If your child is happy to have their own pack of favourite foods irrespective of what the other children are eating, that may be a simpler solution for you in almost every situation.

It is important to ensure that foods are not restricted from a child's diet without a confirmed diagnosis of a food allergy or food intolerance, or other medical reason.

FRIENDS' PARTIES

A completely different approach, given FODMAPs are not currently known to cause damage to the intestine, is to let your child eat what they like at the party. If there's ever a time when you could allow your child to break their diet and eat foods that aren't low-FODMAP, this could be it.

Food allergies and intolerances are common among school-age children, and many host parents will consider this when purchasing foods for their child's party. Nonetheless, it's wise both to inform the host parent of your child's dietary requirements and not to expect them to cater specifically for every child they invite. A good option is always to take the initiative yourself and make equivalent foods to send along with your child to the party, so they can eat your party food and not feel left out.

When speaking with the host parent, emphasise that your child's issue is not an anaphylactic allergy. If they seem willing, you could ask for their help in ensuring your child eats only suitable foods. You could ask them what type of foods will be served (if they've decided yet!), and advise them which (if any) of these are suitable for your child. They may be interested in your suggestions of what types of foods could be offered, or may ask brand names of suitable foods (please visit the Low-FODMAP Diet Shopping Guide available at www.shepherdworks.com.au/shop).

If your child is very symptomatic after eating high-FODMAP foods, explain to your child that they shouldn't have a large amount of food they don't usually eat as it may make them ill or uncomfortable later. A completely different approach, given FODMAPs are not currently known to cause damage to the intestine, is to let your child eat what they like at the party. If there's ever a time when you could allow your child to break their diet and eat foods that aren't low-FODMAP, this could be it.

SLEEPOVERS

It's probable that if your child is sleeping at someone else's home, you or your child must already know them quite well. The host family may be keen to listen and learn about your child's special dietary requirements and to accommodate them as much as possible. To help them do this, you should let them know some suitable dinner and breakfast options, or even better you could send these along with your child (breakfast cereal in a zip-lock bag, for example). You might like to pack up some extra snacks in your child's schoolbag so they have an after-school snack at the host's home and, if necessary, lunch for the next day. If your child sleeps over at this friend's house often, the hosts might be open to you leaving a whole packet of cereal there, and some suitable snacks, too.

SCHOOL AND OTHER CAMPS

You may be able to relax the diet and allow your child to eat the normal menu while they're away on camp, but this isn't an option if your child becomes very unwell with their IBS symptoms. In such instances, it's important to train your child to choose appropriate foods. They should be able to manage quite well in this ideal opportunity to show their independence.

Although most school and club camp organisers are experienced at handling special dietary requirements, the following preparations may make the camping experience more enjoyable for your child – and less of a worry for you.

If the organisers don't already know of your child's needs, be sure not only to document these on the information forms, but also to speak directly with the organiser to convey your child's needs clearly. Make sure they have no questions and check if the staff will be able to ensure that your child's needs are met – both in terms of having suitable foods and not feeling excluded at mealtimes.

You might like to check over the camp menu before your child's departure, indicate to the organisers which meals are already suitable, and work on some reasonable alternatives for those that aren't. You could also provide brand names for suitable snacks and other packaged foods. For meals on the camp menu that aren't suitable, you might like to make equivalent foods and send them to the camp cook, so that your child can eat your matching food and not feel left out.

Remember that the camp organisers will have your contact number and will contact you if any problems arise or your child becomes ill. Do what you can to assist your child to maintain a Low-FODMAP Diet, but be realistic and remember that accidents may happen. Above all, make sure your child enjoys the camp!

FOOD REFUSAL AND OTHER EATING-BEHAVIOUR ISSUES

Children are in the process of developing food likes, dislikes and eating behaviours. Food is central to so many important social interactions – at the family dinner table, in the school playground, at parties. Food should be enjoyed and eating times should be enjoyable – this is important now and also for your child to develop a good relationship with food in the future.

Sometimes children who've been unwell with IBS symptoms recognise that food is the trigger, and this can have a negative impact on their relationship with food. They may refuse to eat specific foods, or even meals. If your child needs to follow a Low-FODMAP Diet and they already have food fears, they may not want to eat even low-FODMAP foods. It can be hard to rationalise with a child and say 'These foods won't make you feel sick' when all they know is that food full stop makes them feel sick.

If you're finding it a challenge to get your child to eat on the Low-FODMAP Diet, I recommend consulting a specialist dietitian who deals with children's eating behaviours and/or food allergies and intolerances for some expert tips. Visit www.daa.asn.au to find a specialist Accredited Practising Dietitian.

> “*I have a daughter 32, who has had problems with her digestion since she was small. Gastroscopy, colonoscopy, x-rays ... changed eating habits ... supplements, vitamins, more books, more recipes, more disappointment and more despair. My daughter now has serious mental health issues as a result of years of not being able to go out to eat and loss of friends, having to cope with the effects of upset digestive system ... the toilets are never close enough. NOTHING made much of a difference. A friend [a nutritionist and dietitian] put us onto your diet/eating plan... AMAZING! It has made such a difference. Now we have the reasons/explanations for what happens to her, it's easier for her to manage too. I can't tell you just how happy it's made me.*”

6. EATING OUT AND TRAVELLING

EATING OUT

When eating out, unless you're dining at a 'FODMAP-aware' restaurant, it's likely that the restaurant's menu will be laden with high-FODMAP foods. Onion, garlic and wheat are regularly used in recipes. Despite this, your special dietary requirements need not be a social sentence. Have the confidence to eat out and enjoy it.

As FODMAPs are not known to cause damage to the intestine, a meal out at a restaurant with friends might be one time you break the diet and eat foods that aren't low-FODMAP. Sometimes the symptoms might be worth it if there's something on the menu that really tempts your tastebuds.

In many instances, though, you may still wish to follow your low-FODMAP needs as much as possible. If you're eating out with friends, they may leave it to you to choose the restaurant. Often, restaurants that specialise in gluten-free are more flexible and open to accommodating other dietary needs. Restaurants that promote their gluten-free menus can be found at www.glutenfreeeatingdirectory.com.au

It's not always possible to choose the restaurant yourself, but even if you do, it's wise to let the staff know about your dietary needs. Often, restaurant staff (even the chef) may not be familiar with FODMAP requirements ...

It's not always possible to choose the restaurant yourself, but even if you do, it's wise to let the staff know about your dietary needs. Often, restaurant staff (even the chef) may not be familiar with FODMAP requirements, so it may be simpler to ask for a 'gluten-free meal with no onion'. If you prefer to be more specific, I recommend asking what ingredients are used in the dish you wish to order. You probably won't be able to speak with the chef directly, so ask the waiters to ask the chef for you – this is important, as wait staff might know a lot, but only the chef knows exactly what has gone into the meal! It can often be helpful to carry a business-card-sized summary of your Low-FODMAP Diet in your wallet and use it when explaining your dietary needs. A dietitian could also help you with this.

Some FODMAP hazards to try to avoid when eating out are:

- stocks, stock cubes and boosters, which can often contain onion and/or garlic
- onion and garlic in risottos and stir-fries
- onion in Greek and other salads – it usually isn't sufficient to just pull the onion out and leave it uneaten on the plate. Request that your salad is onion-free in the first instance.
- dried shallot sprinkled on top of Asian dishes as a garnish
- ready-made sauces and marinades containing garlic and onion
- sausages containing onion

- stuffing inside a roast chicken, which usually consists of wheat breadcrumbs and lots of onion! Seasoning on the chicken skin may also contain onion.
- hot potato chips, which may be coated in flavoured salts (e.g. chicken salt, vegetable salt)
- serves of crème brûlée, panna cotta and ice cream if you *don't* have your lactase enzymes with you
- soy latte made with whole soybean soy milk

Instances where FODMAPs should not really be a problem:

- asparagus, cauliflower or mushrooms in a risotto or stir-fry and so on, which can be easily identified and left uneaten on the plate
- croutons in salads, which you can either eat (as such a small amount is unlikely to cause symptoms) or leave uneaten on the plate
- fish dusted in wheat flour before pan-frying, as the amount of flour is insufficient to cause symptoms
- crumbed chicken, fish, veal, and so on, which for most people won't contain sufficient FODMAPs to cause symptoms. If necessary, scrape some off, but don't be too concerned about removing all of the crumbs.
- wheat as an ingredient in soy sauce, mayonnaise, and so on – these are low-FODMAP items
- serves of crème brûlée, panna cotta and ice cream if you *do* have your lactase enzymes with you.

“ *... after suffering for 29 years I improved dramatically in 24 hours of changing to the FODMAP diet. I still cannot believe the change this has made. It has now been some three weeks and I am still pinching myself to confirm I am not dreaming.*

I live in the UK and I have undergone many examinations, tests and tried numerous medications over the last 29 years and have always been told by the medical community that it is IBS and that there is no useful treatment. It has been very debilitating, painful and at times embarrassing, and has disrupted every aspect of my life.

Although I learnt to cope with it, it was not easy and there have been some very low points. I do not believe that most non-sufferers, including those in the medical community, understand the effects of this condition on the sufferer. ”

TRAVELLING

Around Australia

If you're catering for yourself on your travels within Australia, you'll benefit from knowing the local names for certain foods and also being familiar with the types of foods that are likely to be available and the outlets that are likely to sell them, even though every city and town will differ in the variety of suitable low-FODMAP foods it offers.

If your travels are part of a pre-paid package that includes catering, remember to organise your special meals before you go, as the tour company will be unlikely to have the capacity or resources to prepare meals accommodating your needs after you've commenced the journey. It would be wise to pack some between-meal snacks such as biscuits, bars, cakes, muffins, nuts and seeds; some corn thins, rice cakes or low-FODMAP crackers as a basis for 'building' a lunch; and a low-FODMAP breakfast cereal just in case.

If you're travelling overseas to a country where English isn't spoken, it's wise to take a business-card-sized translated version of your dietary needs in your purse or wallet.

Overseas destinations

Although the Low-FODMAP Diet is now used in many countries around the world, it's still a fairly new dietary concept. You're unlikely to find 'FODMAP Friendly' foods in every country you visit. It would be wise to read the ingredients list on any packaged food – with a translator handy for languages other than English. For label-reading hints (in English) see page 63. When eating in restaurants, don't assume that all meals are prepared with the same ingredients and methods as in Australia.

If you're travelling overseas to a country where English isn't spoken, it's wise to take a business-card-sized translated version of your dietary needs in your purse or wallet. To assist you, you could use an app, or see the translations of eating phrases and low- and high-FODMAP foods by using Google Translate.

7. A HEALTHY LIFESTYLE

ARE YOU A HEALTHY BODY WEIGHT AND SHAPE?

Body mass index (BMI) is a formula that establishes how healthy your weight is for your height. If you fall within the healthy weight range for your height, you're at the lowest risk of developing some common chronic health problems. The BMI is suitable for women and men over the age of eighteen, but is unreliable for people with very muscular physiques (e.g. body builders). If you're of Asian, Maori or Pacific Islander descent, different weight reference ranges may apply (you can find these on the internet).

BMI is calculated using the following formula:

The BMI is suitable for women and men over the age of eighteen, but is unreliable for people with very muscular physiques (e.g. body builders). If you're of Asian, Maori or Pacific Islander descent, different weight reference ranges may apply ...

$$\text{BMI} = (\text{weight in kilograms}) / (\text{height in metres})^2$$

Waist circumference (WC) is a good measure of how much fat you may be carrying around the middle. Measure your waist around the navel using a tape measure and compare the value with those in the table below.

BMI AND WAIST CIRCUMFERENCE INDICATORS FOR AUSTRALIANS

MEASURE	REFERENCE RANGE
BMI	Underweight: < 18.5 kg/m^2 Healthy: 18.5–24.9 kg/m^2 Overweight: 25–29.9 kg/m^2 Obese: $\geq$ 30 kg/m^2
WC	**Men** Normal: < 94.0 cm Overweight: 94.0–101.9 cm Obese: $\geq$ 102.0 cm **Women** Normal: < 80.0 cm Overweight: 80.0–87.9 cm Obese: $\geq$ 88.0 cm

DIETARY GUIDELINES FOR AUSTRALIANS

The 2013 Australian Guide to Healthy Eating provide specific dietary guidelines for men, women and children that can help spell out the fundamentals of healthy eating. The basic principles for adults are outlined below, with recommendations for the Low-FODMAP Diet. It's still well and truly possible to eat healthily while following a Low-FODMAP Diet.

In adjusting, you need to work through and acknowledge your feelings of loss. Know that you don't need to over-eat because you should be able to have more later. With a sensible approach to eating and exercise, you're unlikely to gain weight.

1. **To achieve and maintain a healthy weight, be physically active and choose amounts of nutritious food and drinks to meet your energy needs.**

   No set amount of food and exercise is right for everybody, and no single weight is right for those of the same height, sex and age. Additionally, children and adolescents need to ensure they eat sufficient nutritious foods to assist with optimal growth and development. All people (children, adolescents, adults) should be physically active to help muscle strength and achieve a healthy weight. A great daily target for adults is walking 10,000 steps per day. Other hints are available at: www.healthyactive.gov.au

   Be aware of the possibility of gaining weight when you commence the Low-FODMAP Diet. In the adjustment period, some people find they over-eat the foods that are low in FODMAPs, 'just because they can' e.g. wheat-free biscuits and cakes. There are many restrictions on what you *can't* have, so that many overindulge on what they *can*. These feelings are common, but can lead to weight gain.

   In adjusting, you need to work through and acknowledge your feelings of loss. Know that you don't need to over-eat because you should be able to have more later. With a sensible approach to eating and exercise, you're unlikely to gain weight.

   Use the BMI and WC charts on page 77 to see how you shape up.

2. **Enjoy a wide variety of nutritious foods from the five food groups every day.**

   The five food groups are vegetables, fruit, grain foods, protein foods and dairy foods. Eating a wide variety of foods is your best insurance for meeting your recommended requirements for vitamins, minerals, protein, energy and fibre. We need these each day for our optimum health. You should also drink plenty of water.

3. **Limit your intake of foods containing saturated fat, added salt, added sugars and alcohol.**

   Limit your intake of foods high in saturated fat, such as many biscuits, cakes, pastries, pies, processed meats, commercial burgers, pizza, fried foods, potato chips, crisps and other savoury snacks. Replace high-fat foods that contain predominantly saturated fats, such as butter, cream, cooking margarine and palm oil, with foods that contain predominantly polyunsaturated and monounsaturated fats, such as oils, margarine, nut butters (low-FODMAP) and pastes, and avocado. Low-fat diets are not usually recommended for children under two years old.

Limit your intake of foods and drinks containing added salt. Read labels to choose the lower sodium options among similar foods and don't add salt to foods during cooking or at the table.

Limit your intake of foods and drinks containing added sugars, such as confectionery, sugar-sweetened soft drinks and cordials, fruit drinks, vitamin waters, and energy and sports drinks.

If you choose to drink alcohol, limit your intake following the government standard drinks guide and choose low-FODMAP types (see page 92). For women who are pregnant, planning a pregnancy or breastfeeding, the safest recommendation is not to drink alcohol.

4. **Encourage, support and promote breastfeeding.**
5. **Care for your food; prepare and store it safely.**

“*I just wanted to tell you that your research into the Low-FODMAP Diet changed my life. Since I started following it, I can get out of bed every morning . . . something I wasn't able to do for the past five years. I have energy, and I'm excited about life. This is all thanks to you.*

Thank you for devoting your time to researching how to help people with IBS. It has literally saved me.”

EATING WELL

Vegetables

Enjoy plenty of vegetables of different types and colours, as this provides us with a variety of vitamins and minerals. Try to eat five serves of low-FODMAP vegetables each day, preferably from each of the groups below:

- dark-green leafy vegetables – spinach, silverbeet, bok choy, choy sum
- orange–yellow vegetables – pumpkin (restrict butternut), carrots, sweet potato (limit), squash
- starchy vegetables – potato, sweet potato, parsnip
- others – beans, lettuce, zucchini, capsicum, swede, turnips, cucumber, eggplant.

As you work through the reintroduction process of Step Two, you may find you can tolerate an every greater variety of vegetables. If you find during Step Two that you can tolerate a particular type of FODMAP, don't forget to include any of the vegetables high in that FODMAP (shown in the tables on pages 17–22), as tolerated. You will also notice that the recipes show you how you can include new vegetables according to any FODMAP you find you may tolerate during the reintroduction process. Legumes and lentils are also included in this vegetable food group. These are high-protein plant food, but as they contain the FODMAPs GOS and fructans they won't be suitable for everyone. These are restricted during Step One of the Low-FODMAP Diet however, for vegetarians, especially vegans, they are a valuable protein. For vegans and those who tolerate the GOS challenge (page 37), I recommend trying small amounts over a few meals rather than a large serve in one meal. Also, lentils contain less FODMAPs than legume beans, so you may find you tolerate these better.

Legumes include baked beans, lentils, soybeans, kidney beans, broad beans, mung beans, chickpeas, lima beans, navy beans and borlotti beans. Legumes are often more convenient in their canned form but also widely available dried. If you consume these on your Low-FODMAP Diet, I recommend trying small amounts over a few meals rather than one large meal based on legumes. Note that cooking and draining lentils lowers their FODMAP content.

Fruit

Fruits are a great snack idea and really nutritious. Try to include two pieces per day from the following low-FODMAP suggestions during Step One of the Low-FODMAP Diet. Refer to pages 24 for fruits containing high levels of a FODMAP that you may find you tolerate after completing Step Two of the Low- FODMAP Diet – you may be able to expand the range of fruits you can enjoy! Remember to spread out your fruit intake out to be the equivalent of one piece of fruit at a time, every 2–3 hours (as described on page 17):

- low-FODMAP fruits rich in vitamin C – oranges, mandarins, lemon, lime, strawberries, raspberries, blueberries, pineapple, kiwifruit, pawpaw, tomatoes or
- low-FODMAP fruits rich in vitamin A – cantaloupe, pawpaw, tomatoes or
- other low-FODMAP fruits – banana, grapes, honeydew melon or passionfruit.

Grain foods

Enjoy grain (cereal) foods, such as low-FODMAP breads, cereals, pasta, noodles (see page 27), also rice, polenta, buckwheat, sorghum, millet, oats, quinoa. Choose wholegrain varieties in preference to refined varieties (e.g. sugar and white starches) as wholegrain varieties offer much more nutrition and help minimise risk of chronic disease. For example, where possible choose brown rice rather than white; oat, quinoa porridge or wholegrain cereal rather than puffed rice or flakes of corn. These grain foods contain carbohydrates, which give us energy. Wheat-, rye- and barley-based breads, cereals, pasta and crackers are high in FODMAPs when eaten in large amounts, and are recommended to be restricted during Step One. However, if you tolerate the Fructan A challenge (page 37), you may find that you can include these in your diet again, according to your own tolerance levels.

Protein foods

Low-FODMAP protein foods include plain lean meats and poultry, fish, eggs and tofu. Nuts, seeds and legumes, are all also considered protein foods, however these can be higher in FODMAPs. During Step One, restrict cashews, pistachios, legumes and lentils but enjoy other nuts and seeds in moderation. Once you complete the reintroduction process, you may find you can include more of these high-FODMAP foods in your diet. It is recommended that adults eat between 1–2 serves of lean protein foods per day.

These high protein foods are also good sources of iron. Iron helps your body carry oxygen in the blood, and women need more because of blood losses during menstruation. Red meats and offal are excellent sources of iron (e.g. beef, lamb, kidney, liver and liver-based pâté). Good sources include chicken, sardines, salmon, tuna, pork and eggs. Iron from animal sources is called haem iron and is more easily absorbed by the body than iron from plant foods. Women can meet their daily iron needs by eating an average serve (120 grams) of beef or lamb, two serves (½ cup each) of leafy green vegetables, a handful (about ⅓ cup) of low-FODMAP nuts, 1 cup of low-FODMAP wholegrain cereal or two slices of multigrain low-FODMAP bread.

It is still recommended to limit saturated fat, however 'low fat' is no longer the centre of the healthy fat philosophy. Many naturally occurring fats are considered valuable sources of energy and nutrients, and are encouraged in the diet.

Milk-based foods and beverages

Low-FODMAP milk-based foods and beverages include lactose-free milk, lactose-free yoghurt and all formed/block/hard/yellow cheeses. A full selection is on page 26 and these can be enjoyed during Step One of the Low-FODMAP Diet. Reduced fat varieties are preferable. If you tolerate lactose during the reintroduction process (page 37), you can enjoy regular varieties of milk and yoghurt (low-FODMAP flavours), and soft cheeses.

Milk-based products are all excellent sources of calcium, which the body uses to build bones and teeth, and to keep them hard and strong. Osteoporosis is a condition of weak, brittle bones and it can affect males and females but it is most common in elderly women. To help minimise the risk of osteoporosis, we are all encouraged to include two to three serves of milk-based products in our diet every day. Milk based products are the richest sources of calcium however other foods such as sardines, tuna and salmon with bones (if canned), calcium-fortified plant-based milk drinks, almonds and Brazil nuts provide smaller amounts of calcium.

If you're lactose-intolerant, choose lactose-free cow's milk (which has as much calcium as regular milk) or choose a *calcium-fortified* soy milk made from soy protein or soy extract (not whole soybeans), or rice or oat milk. Soy, rice and oat milks do not naturally contain high levels of calcium, so check the ingredients list and food labels to ensure calcium has been added so that it is an equivalent to regular milk.

Fats and oils

Over the past decade, the messages around healthy eating of fat have changed. It is still recommended to limit saturated fat, however 'low fat' is no longer the centre of the healthy fat philosophy. Many naturally occurring fats are considered valuable sources of energy and nutrients, and are encouraged in the diet.

To understand the terminology of fats, here is a description of the four common types of fats in foods:

Trans fatty acids tend to act like saturated fats and are not desirable in the diet. These fats can be formed in the processing of some fats and oils.

- Saturated fats are usually of animal origin, with exceptions being coconut and palm oil. Saturated fats tend to be solid at room temperature. Major sources of saturated fat in the diet include:
  - Fat found naturally in foods such as meat, poultry, milk, cheese, and coconut and palm oil
  - Fat added to cooking and preparation at home, such as butter on bread, cream in cooking, ghee/lard to fry foods
  - Fat added in commercial processing of foods such as cakes, pastries, biscuits, snacks, fatty smallgoods and sausages and other processed foods
- Monounsaturated fats are found in greatest amounts in plant sources. Monounsaturated fat is one of the types of fats that is considered healthful, and is found in foods such as olive margarines and oils, canola, avocados, peanuts, macadamias, peanut butter and hazelnuts.
- Polyunsaturated fats are also considered a better fat source and consist of two main classes.
  - Omega-6 plant sources including oils such as sunflower and safflower oils, polyunsaturated margarine, some nuts including walnuts and Brazil nuts, and seeds such as sesame, pumpkin (pepitas), and sunflower seeds.
  - Omega-3 found in polyunsaturated oils and margarines (e.g. canola, soyabean, linseed), however the main sources are from oily fish (e.g. herring, salmon, tuna, mackerel, sardines, gemfish).

- Trans fatty acids tend to act like saturated fats and are not desirable in the diet. These fats can be formed in the processing of some fats and oils. Sources of trans fats include hydrogenated vegetable fats that are used in foods such as deep-fried foods, some take-away meals and baked goods, such as pies, pastries, cakes and biscuits.

So, the gist of the good fat/bad fat message is:

- Saturated fat has been linked with heart disease, diabetes and high cholesterol levels
- Limit intake of processed foods containing saturated fat e.g. cakes, pastries, smallgoods and snack foods
- Replace saturated fat with poly- and/or monounsaturated fats is recommended
- Low fat is not recommended – instead use whole foods naturally containing polyunsaturated and monounsaturated fats including avocado, nuts, seeds, olive oil and oily fish (e.g. herring, salmon, sardines, mackerel). If you have goals for weight control, fat has more energy per gram than protein or fat, so although fats should still be included, this will need to be considered in any weight loss eating plan.
- Choose whole foods in preference over white/refined/overly processed foods so you can enjoy all the other nutritional goodness the food can provide.

Limiting salt

Salt can cause high blood pressure in some people. The major source of salt in the diet is processed foods, but many people are in the habit of adding salt during cooking or at the table. Ensure you taste your food before adding salt – your food may be flavoursome enough without it. Instead of adding salt, flavour your food with low-FODMAP alternatives such as those described on page 91.

Cutting down on sugar

Sugar and some sugary foods and drinks (such as lollies and soft drinks) are full of energy (kilojoules) but contain no vitamins and minerals. Many foods such as cakes, biscuits and chocolate are high in sugar and fat, and mostly low in fibre. Excessive sugar can cause dental caries, and can contribute to weight gain by providing excess energy in the diet.

Try to choose snacks with little or no added sugar, such as fresh low-FODMAP fruit, vegetable sticks and low-FODMAP dips, low-fat cheese, low-FODMAP nuts, unsweetened yoghurt or popcorn.

Sugar and some sugary foods and drinks (such as lollies and soft drinks) are full of energy (kilojoules) but contain no vitamins and minerals. Many foods such as cakes, biscuits and chocolate are high in sugar and fat, and mostly low in fibre. Excessive sugar can cause dental caries, and can contribute to a high-energy diet, leading to weight gain and being overweight.

Importance of fibre

Dietary fibre is the part of plants that can't be broken down by our body. It's found in grains, fruits, vegetables, legumes, nuts and seeds. Meat, eggs, milk, cheese and fats do not naturally contain any dietary fibre. It's recommended that women consume 25 grams and men 30 grams of fibre per day. Dietary fibre is one of the essential components of our diet, but most people don't include enough in their daily diet. As part of a healthy diet, fibre has been shown to assist regular bowel habits, help with weight control, lower blood cholesterol and improve diabetes management. Adequate fibre in the diet has also been shown to reduce the risk of bowel cancer. When you restrict wheat intake, it can result in a reduced intake of usual breads and cereals, and your diet can become low in fibre. Fortunately, there are plenty of wholegrain high-fibre low-FODMAP breads and cereals that you can enjoy, and still meet your daily fibre target. See the fibre hints on the following page and also pages 272–273 to guide you. If you need a hand planning your diet to obtain enough fibre, have a chat with your dietitian.

LOW- VERSUS HIGH-FIBRE LOW-FODMAP FOOD CHOICES

Boost your fibre intake in your Low-FODMAP Diet by choosing wholegrain, unrefined cereal and grain foods where possible. Choose fresh fruit instead of juice and also leave the skin on your fruit and vegetables where possible. See the difference that just a few wise choices can make to your fibre intake, by comparing the high-fibre column with the low-fibre column in the table below:

LOW-FIBRE MENU*	FIBRE (GRAMS PER SERVE)	HIGH-FIBRE MENU*	FIBRE (GRAMS PER SERVE)
Breakfast		**Breakfast**	
Orange juice	0	Whole orange	2.4
Puffed rice	0	Gluten-free Weet-Bix	3.1
Milk	0	Milk	0
White low-FODMAP bread, toasted	1.2	Grainy low-FODMAP bread, toasted	1.6
Lunch		**Lunch**	
Cheese sandwich, white low-FODMAP bread	2.4	Cheese and salad sandwich, grainy low-FODMAP bread	4.0
Plain wheat-free cake	0	Pecan and cinnamon muffin	1.8
Dinner		**Dinner**	
Steak	0	Steak	0
Chips	2.5	Baked potato (with skin)	4
Fried Egg	0	Mixed low-FODMAP vegetables	4.5
Ice cream	0	Lactose-free yoghurt with low-FODMAP fruit salad	2.6
Between meals		**Between meals**	
Chocolate	0	Low-FODMAP fruit	2.5
Rice cakes with jam	0.5	Rice cakes with crunchy peanut butter	2.5
Total fibre	**6.6**	**Total fibre**	**29**

*approximates used

PART 2: TWO-STEP LOW-FODMAP RECIPES

In the following section of the book, you will be able to immerse your tastebuds in the wonderful flavours of the Low-FODMAP Diet – in fact, in BOTH steps of the Low-FODMAP Diet!

The main recipe has been written to cater for the first phase of the Low-FODMAP Diet – where foods containing high amounts of each type of FODMAP are limited. However, you will find handy notes at the bottom of most recipes, identifying additional ingredients (or changes to ingredients) that you can use in step two if you have discovered, during the reintroduction process, that you can tolerate a particular type of FODMAP.

So, you can be excited to know that all the recipes will suit you through your journey on the Low-FODMAP Diet from step one (strict restriction) to step two (liberalisation that is individualised).

Readers please note: all base recipes have been formulated using ingredients known to be low-FODMAP at the time of publishing. Some recipes use small amounts of foods containing moderate levels of FODMAPs, which when used in the small quantities specified will be low in FODMAPs, based on information at the time of publishing. Recipes have not been laboratory tested for FODMAP levels. Whilst every effort has been taken to design low-FODMAP recipes recommended serving sizes, and 'if you can tolerate' Step Two recipe extras, assess your own level of tolerance.

IF YOU CAN TOLERATE

For most recipes, I have suggested ways to include additional ingredients to the base recipe, according to different types of FODMAPs. For example, after completing the reintroduction process if you know that you can tolerate mannitol, you may like to add mushrooms to Spaghetti Bolognese (see page 140). Similarly if you can tolerate fructans after undergoing the reintroduction process of Step Two, then you could use garlic instead of garlic-infused olive oil. The suggested amounts are to be used as a guide – adjust to your own tolerance levels of that FODMAP. Enjoy your individualised recipes!

With all recipes requiring the use of an oven, the oven temperature is for a fan-forced oven. If you don't have a fan-forced oven, individual variation can occur across ovens, however a general rule of thumb is to increase the temperature stated in the recipe by 10°C.

A few specific notes about low FODMAP cooking:

- **Stock:** Most stocks contain onion or garlic. Try to choose one that is onion free. If garlic is present, the amount is typically minimal and should be suitable for most people on step one (and two) of the Low-FODMAP Diet.
- **Lactose-free cream:** unfortunately lactose free cream does not whip. So, if whipping is required, I have used regular cream and indicated that people with lactose intolerance should only have a small serve.
- **Soy flour:** contains the FODMAPs fructans and GOS. However as only a small amount is used in some recipes, the amount present per serve has been found not to cause IBS symptoms in most people. Assess your individual tolerance. Additionally, it is not recommended you taste the raw mix (e.g. cake batter, pancake batter, biscuit dough) – soy flour has a bitter taste when raw, which disappears when cooked.
- **Garlic-infused olive oil:** many recipes call for the use of garlic-infused olive oil. This is a great product, available in supermarkets and speciality stores – you get the garlic flavour without the grief! Please use only commercially prepared garlic-infused olive oil – do not make your own at home as it poses some potentially serious health risks. Commercially prepared garlic-infused olive oil is safe to use.

LOW-FODMAP FLAVOUR BOOSTERS!

The recipes in this book are bursting with flavour. I'm sure you won't notice that I haven't used onion or garlic. The trick is to boost your food with the fabulous spectrum of flavours that herbs and spices can deliver. Try using any of the following herbs (fresh is best!) and spices:

- Allspice
- Asafoetida
- Basil
- Bay leaves
- Caraway
- Cardamom
- Cayenne pepper
- Chervil
- Chilli powder
- Chives
- Cinnamon
- Clove
- Coriander
- Cumin
- Curry leaves
- Dill
- Fenugreek
- Galangal
- Ginger
- Juniper berry
- Kaffir lime leaves
- Lavender
- Lemon basil
- Lemongrass
- Lemon thyme
- Marjoram
- Mustard
- Nutmeg
- Oregano
- Paprika
- Parsley
- Pepper
- Peppermint
- Rosemary
- Saffron
- Sage
- Star anise
- Tarragon
- Thyme
- Vanilla

If you are missing the taste of onion or garlic, here are some great tips for you to still enjoy the flavour without the grief! Many onion- and garlic-infused olive oils are now available in the olive-oil section of supermarkets. It is recommended to only use commercially-made infused olive oils. Also, you can enjoy delicious onion and garlic flavour by using chives (including garlic chives) and the green part of spring onions as these are low-FODMAP. Enjoy!

BEVERAGES ON A LOW-FODMAP DIET

FODMAPs are not exclusive to foods. They can also be present in drinks, both alcoholic and non-alcoholic, as indicated below.

High-FODMAP non-alcoholic drinks

Fruit juices:

- apple juice, pear juice (excess fructose and sorbitol)
- mango juice, tropical juice (excess fructose)
- pomegranate juice (fructans)
- apricot nectar, peach juice (sorbitol)
- more than ⅓–½ cup cranberry juice, orange juice, pineapple juice or other juices made from 'balanced' fruits (due to high fructose load)

Vegetable juices:

- those with onion, or large amounts of beetroot (fructans) or celery (mannitol)

Soft drinks:

- fructose-sweetened: all
- sugar-sweetened: more than 2 small glasses per sitting of cola, lemonade, ginger ale and other soft drinks (high fructose load)

Milk:

- cow's, goat's or sheep's milk (lactose)
- soy milk made from whole soybeans (fructans and GOS)

Low-FODMAP non-alcoholic drinks

Fruit juices:

- no more than ⅓–½ cup of cranberry, orange, pineapple or other juices made from 'balanced' fruits

Vegetable juices:

- all should be fine except those with onion or large amounts of beetroot or celery

Sugar-sweetened drinks (e.g. soft drinks):

- sugar-sweetened: no more than 2 small glasses per sitting. Although sugar (sucrose) contains a balance of fructose and glucose, soft drinks consumed in large amounts will provide too great a fructose load.
- diet: the artificial sweeteners used in soft drinks are not polyols, and do not contribute to IBS symptoms

Milk

- lactose-free milk, rice milk, oat milk or soy milk (only if made from soybean extract)

Other

- water, ginger beer, bitters, tonic water, mineral water, soda water, cordial (check tolerance of apple and mango flavours)

High-FODMAP alcoholic drinks

Wines:

- most sweet white wines – e.g. riesling, moscato
- most dessert wines – e.g. sherry, port, muscat, tokay, ice wine, sauternes, botrytis-style wines

Spirits:

- most rums

Ciders:

- most ciders, usually based on either apple or pear juice

Low-FODMAP alcoholic drinks

Of course I mean only in moderation – see Chapter 7, 'A healthy lifestyle', for more.

Wines:

- most dry white wines – e.g. chardonnay, sauvignon blanc, semillon, marsanne, verdelho, pinot grigio
- most red wines – e.g. pinot noir, shiraz, cabernet sauvignon, merlot, sangiovese, grenache, tempranillo, rosé
- many other wines – e.g. sake

Beers:

- ale, lager, stout – even if the beer is made from wheat, the amount of wheat present should not be a problem

Spirits:

- vodka and gin are good choices
- in moderation, most varieties of the following are also likely to be low-FODMAP choices, just be sure to choose your mixer wisely:
    - bourbon
    - brandy
    - cognac
    - gin
    - grappa
    - ouzo
    - sambuca
    - scotch
    - tequila
    - vodka
    - whisky

BREAKFAST

SCRAMBLED EGGS ON CORNBREAD

- 10 large eggs
- 85 mL (1/3 cup) lactose-free cream
- salt and freshly ground black pepper
- 1 teaspoon butter

CORNBREAD

- 70 g (½ cup) fine rice flour
- 45 g (¼ cup) gluten-free cornflour
- 35 g (¼ cup) tapioca flour
- 190 g (1 cup) instant polenta
- 2 teaspoons baking powder (gluten-free if on a gluten-free diet)
- 1 teaspoon bicarbonate of soda
- 1 teaspoon xanthan gum
- 1 teaspoon salt
- 2 eggs, lightly beaten
- 250 mL (1 cup) lactose-free milk
- 1 tablespoon olive oil
- 1 small red chilli, seeded and finely chopped
- 50 g (½ cup) grated parmesan
- 1 teaspoon coarsely ground salt (extra)

SPICY SAUCE

- 3 teaspoons garlic-infused olive oil *
- ¼ teaspoon ground cumin
- 1 teaspoon smoked paprika
- 200 g crushed canned tomatoes
- 1–2 teaspoons finely chopped mint
- salt and freshly ground black pepper

This recipe has three parts but each is easily made ahead of time, with the last steps done when you are ready to serve.

To make the Cornbread, preheat the oven to 180°C. Lightly grease a 24 cm × 10 cm loaf tin and line with baking paper.

Place flours, polenta, baking powder, bicarbonate of soda, xanthan gum and salt in a bowl and mix well with a whisk to ensure they are well combined.

In a separate small bowl, combine the eggs, milk, olive oil, chilli and parmesan. Add to the flour mixture, mixing well. Pour into the prepared tin, smooth the top with the back of a wet metal spoon and sprinkle with coarsely ground salt.

Bake for 35–45 minutes or until a skewer inserted into the centre comes out clean. Remove from the oven and allow to cool in the tin for 10 minutes. Turn out on to a wire rack to cool fully and slice.

To make the Spicy Sauce, heat the olive oil in a small frying pan over a medium heat. Add the cumin and paprika and heat for 30 seconds, stirring, to develop the flavours. Add the crushed tomatoes and cook for 2 minutes, until it is slightly reduced. Stir through the mint and season to taste. Set aside to cool slightly while you cook the eggs.

To make the Scrambled Eggs, whisk together the eggs and cream in a large bowl. Season with salt and pepper.

Melt the butter in a medium-sized frying pan over a low heat. Pour in the egg mixture and use a wooden spoon to gently push the egg mixture around the edges and into the middle of the pan every 10 seconds to prevent sticking. Cook for 3–5 minutes or until just set; the texture will be creamy and a little runny.

Meanwhile, toast the cornbread.

To serve, place the scrambled eggs on the cornbread and spoon over some spicy sauce.

SERVES 4–6

** Please refer to note on garlic-infused olive oil under heading 'A few specific notes about low-FODMAP cooking', page 89.*

IF YOU CAN TOLERATE

LACTOSE, *use* ***regular*** *milk and cream rather than lactose-free.*

FRUCTANS, *consider one of the following: ½ clove* ***garlic****, crushed and sautéed in olive oil, rather than garlic-infused olive oil; or substitute 1 cup (150 g) plain* ***wheat flour*** *for the rice and tapioca flours and cornflour, and omit xanthan gum (if you are not also gluten-free).*

VANILLA 'PORRIDGE' WITH STRAWBERRY AND RHUBARB COMPOTE AND GRANOLA

GRANOLA

- 8 roasted hazelnuts
- 1 tablespoon sunflower seeds
- 1 tablespoon pumpkin seeds (pepitas)
- ½ teaspoon ground cinnamon
- ½ teaspoon mixed spice
- 3 tablespoons brown sugar

STRAWBERRY AND RHUBARB COMPOTE

- 250 mL (1 cup) water
- 75–110 g (⅓–½ cup) caster sugar
- 2 stalks rhubarb, cut into 2 cm lengths
- 150 g strawberries, hulled and halved

VANILLA 'PORRIDGE'

- 750 mL (3 cups) lactose-free milk
- 75 g (⅓ cup) caster sugar
- 2 teaspoons vanilla bean paste
- 130 g (⅔ cup) instant polenta

To make the Granola, preheat the oven to 180°C. Line a baking tray with baking paper.

Coarsely grind all the ingredients and spread over the baking tray to a thickness of 5 mm.

Bake for 5 minutes until lightly toasted. Allow to cool completely. Store in an airtight container if not using immediately.

To make the Compote, heat the water and sugar in a medium-sized saucepan over a medium–high heat. Stir until the sugar dissolves, then reduce the heat to medium–low. Add the fruit to the saucepan and cook, stirring regularly until the strawberries and rhubarb soften and break down. Cook until the mixture thickens to your desired consistency. Remove from the heat and allow to cool slightly.

To make the Vanilla 'Porridge', heat the milk, sugar and vanilla bean paste in a medium-sized saucepan until almost boiling. Add the polenta, and stir until the mixture boils. Reduce the heat to low, and stir constantly for a further 3–5 minutes until the polenta is cooked and thickened to the consistency of porridge.

Remove from the heat, pour into four bowls and top with the compote and a sprinkling of granola.

SERVES 4

IF YOU CAN TOLERATE

SORBITOL, *you may substitute* ***blackberries*** *for rhubarb.*

EXCESS FRUCTOSE, *you may substitute* ***boysenberries*** *for rhubarb.*

LACTOSE, *use* ***regular*** *rather than lactose-free milk.*

CORN FRITTERS WITH HERBED RICOTTA, AVOCADO AND TOMATOES

- 200 g cherry tomatoes, halved
- 1 tablespoon chopped flat-leaf parsley
- 2 tablespoons extra virgin olive oil, plus extra to serve (optional)
- salt and freshly ground black pepper
- 1 egg, lightly beaten
- 2 tablespoons lactose-free milk
- 70 g (½ cup) fine rice flour
- 45 g (¼ cup) gluten-free cornflour
- 2 tablespoons soy flour *
- 140 g canned corn kernels
- 1 tablespoon finely chopped chives
- 1 tablespoon canola oil
- 1 avocado, chopped into large pieces
- mint leaves, to serve

HERBED RICOTTA

- 4 tablespoons ricotta
- 1 tablespoon chopped mint
- salt and freshly ground black pepper

** Please refer to note on soy flour under heading 'A few specific notes about low-FODMAP cooking', page 89.*

To make the Herbed Ricotta, combine the ricotta and mint in a bowl and season to taste.

To make the Corn Fritters, combine the tomatoes and parsley in a small bowl and add the olive oil. Season to taste. Set aside.

In a small jug, combine the egg and milk.

Place the flours, corn and chives in a bowl and stir until well combined. Season with salt and pepper. Make a well in the middle, add the egg and milk mixture, stir well to combine and set aside to rest for 10 minutes.

Heat the canola oil in a medium-sized frying pan over a medium-high heat. Place spoonfuls of the batter into the hot pan, using 2 tablespoons batter per fritter. Cook for 1–2 minutes or until the bottoms are golden brown, then turn over and flatten slightly with the back of the spatula. Cook for a further 1–2 minutes or until cooked through and golden brown. Transfer the fritters to a plate lined with paper towel and repeat until the batter is used up.

To serve, place 2 warm fritters on a plate, top with tomatoes, avocado and 1 tablespoon herbed ricotta. Drizzle with olive oil and serve with mint leaves, if desired.

SERVES 4

IF YOU CAN TOLERATE

MANNITOL, *you may add* ***sautéed mushrooms*** *with the tomatoes.*

LACTOSE, *use* ***regular*** *rather than lactose-free milk.*

FRUCTANS, *consider one of the following: substitute* ***spring onions*** *for chives; or use 115 g (¾ cup) plain* ***wheat flour*** *instead of rice, corn and soy flours (if you are not also gluten-free).*

SALMON OMELETTE WITH LEMON CRÈME FRAÎCHE

- 2 eggs
- 1 tablespoon finely chopped chives
- salt and freshly ground black pepper
- 2 teaspoons olive oil, plus extra to serve (optional)
- 25 g smoked salmon, cut into strips
- dill sprigs, to serve
- 1 teaspoon capers, to serve
- rocket leaves, to serve

LEMON CRÈME FRAÎCHE

- 2 tablespoons crème fraîche
- 1 teaspoon finely grated lemon zest

To make the Lemon Crème Fraîche, combine the crème fraîche and lemon zest in a small bowl.

To make the Salmon Omelette, whisk together the eggs and chives, and season with salt and pepper.

Heat the olive oil in a small frying pan over a medium heat. Pour in the eggs and cook until almost set on top. Use an egg slide to loosen the edges, and shake the omelette loose. Spread the smoked salmon strips over half of the omelette and fold over the other half to encase the filling. Continue to cook until set. Remove from the heat and serve with the lemon crème fraîche, a sprinkling of dill, a few capers and some rocket leaves. Drizzle with olive oil, if desired.

SERVES 1

IF YOU CAN TOLERATE

FRUCTANS, *substitute* ***spring onions*** *for chives.*

BUTTERMILK PANCAKES WITH BLUEBERRY COMPOTE

BLUEBERRY COMPOTE

- 125 mL (½ cup) water
- 110 g (½ cup) caster sugar
- 300 g (2 punnets) blueberries
- 1 teaspoon finely grated lemon zest

BUTTERMILK PANCAKES

- 1 egg
- 185 mL (¾ cup) buttermilk †
- 70 g (½ cup) fine rice flour
- 50 g (⅓ cup) gluten-free cornflour
- 20 g (¼ cup) soy flour *
- 2½ tablespoons caster sugar
- 1½ teaspoons gluten-free baking powder
- 1 tablespoon melted butter
- cooking oil spray
- 125 mL (½ cup) lactose-free cream, optional

† If lactose intolerant, add a squeeze of fresh lemon juice to lactose-free milk, stir, allow to curdle slightly and use in place of the buttermilk.

** Please refer to note on soy flour under heading 'A few specific notes about low-FODMAP cooking',* *page 89.*

To make the Blueberry Compote, combine the water and sugar in a medium-sized saucepan over a medium–high heat. Stir until the sugar dissolves, then lower the heat to medium–low. Add the blueberries and stir until the berries soften. The fruit mix should be thickened. Remove from the heat and allow to cool slightly. Stir through the lemon zest.

To make the Buttermilk Pancakes, whisk together the egg and buttermilk in a small jug.

Combine the flours, sugar and baking powder in a bowl and whisk to ensure it's well mixed. Make a well in the centre and pour in the egg and milk mixture, mixing well. Gradually draw in the flour to make a smooth batter. Stir in the melted butter, cover and set aside for 15 minutes.

Heat a large non-stick frying pan over a low heat, then spray with cooking oil spray. Add ¼ cup batter to the pan and tilt to spread the mixture to a pancake of 8–10 cm in diameter. Cook for 1–2 minutes or until bubbles start to appear.

Turn and cook for 1–2 minutes or until lightly golden. Transfer to a plate, keep warm in a low oven, and repeat with the remaining batter.

Serve the pancakes with a few spoonfuls of the compote and a drizzle of lactose-free cream, if using.

SERVES 4

IF YOU CAN TOLERATE

SORBITOL, *you may substitute* ***blackberries*** *for blueberries.*

EXCESS FRUCTOSE, *you may substitute* ***boysenberries*** *for blueberries.*

LACTOSE, *use* ***regular*** *rather than lactose-free cream.*

FRUCTANS, *you may substitute 190 g (1¼ cups) plain* ***wheat flour*** *for the rice, soy and cornflours (if you are not also gluten-free).*

SPANISH OMELETTE

- 2 teaspoons canola oil
- ¼ cup onion- and garlic-free chorizo, roughly chopped, or shredded cooked chicken
- ¼ red capsicum, diced
- ½ small tomato, diced
- 1 tablespoon finely sliced spring onion, green part only
- 2 eggs
- 2 tablespoons grated tasty cheese
- ½ teaspoon smoked paprika
- ¼ teaspoon chilli powder (optional)
- 2 teaspoons chopped parsley, plus extra to garnish
- ½ teaspoon thyme
- salt and freshly ground black pepper
- extra virgin olive oil

Heat the canola oil in a small frying pan over a medium heat. Add the chorizo, capsicum, tomato and spring onion and cook for 2–3 minutes, or until the capsicum softens.

Whisk the eggs, cheese, paprika, chilli, if using, parsley, thyme, salt and pepper in a small mixing bowl. Pour into the pan and tilt the pan to ensure an even coating over the chorizo. Cook until the egg is almost set on top. Use an egg slide to loosen the edges, and shake the omelette loose. Flip and continue to heat until cooked through (or place the pan – excluding the handle – under a hot grill until the omelette is set and turning golden brown). Garnish the omelette with the extra parsley and olive oil.

SERVES 1

IF YOU CAN TOLERATE

MANNITOL, *sauté sliced* ***mushrooms*** *with the chorizo.*

FRUCTANS, *use* ***regular chorizo,*** *not one that is garlic- and onion-free.*

LIGHT MEALS

KINGFISH SASHIMI WITH JALAPEÑO AND SOY SAUCE

- 200 g kingfish fillets
- 1–2 jalapeño peppers, seeded and thinly sliced
- gluten-free soy sauce (optional)

Using a sharp knife, cut the kingfish into 2 mm thick slices. Arrange on a serving platter, layering the pieces in a linear fashion down the centre of the platter.

Place a slice of jalapeño pepper in the middle of each piece of sashimi. Serve with chopsticks and individual plates, offering soy sauce.

SERVES 4–6

PUMPKIN, PECAN AND BLUE CHEESE SALAD

- 300 g Jap pumpkin, peeled and cut into 3 cm cubes
- garlic-infused olive oil *
- 3 cups rocket
- 3 cups baby spinach leaves
- 50 g (½ cup) pecans, roughly chopped
- 2 tablespoons pumpkin seeds (pepitas)
- 50 g mild blue cheese, crumbled
- 2 tablespoons extra virgin olive oil
- 1 tablespoon good-quality sweet balsamic vinegar

** Please refer to note on garlic-infused olive oil under heading 'A few specific notes about low-FODMAP cooking', page 89.*

Preheat the oven to 180°C.

Place the pumpkin on a baking tray, drizzle over some garlic-infused olive oil and toss to coat well. Bake for 35–45 minutes or until the pumpkin is cooked and turning golden brown at the edges. Remove from the oven, cover the tray with foil and allow to cool to room temperature. Transfer to the refrigerator to cool completely.

When ready to serve, in a large salad bowl, combine the rocket, spinach, pecans, pepitas, blue cheese and pumpkin.

In a small bowl, combine the extra virgin olive oil and balsamic vinegar. Stir well to combine and pour over the salad. Toss well. Serve immediately.

SERVES 4

INDIVIDUAL CAESAR SALADS WITH GARLIC-FLAVOURED CROUTONS

- 60 g short-cut rindless bacon, cut into thin strips
- 2 tablespoons garlic-infused olive oil *
- 2 slices white gluten-free low-FODMAP bread, cut into 1 cm cubes
- 4 large eggs
- 2 baby cos lettuces, leaves separated, washed and dried
- 60 g fresh parmesan, shaved

DRESSING

- 85 g (1/3 cup) whole-egg mayonnaise
- 1 teaspoon lemon juice
- 3 anchovy fillets
- 1–1½ teaspoons Dijon mustard
- ½ teaspoon brown sugar
- salt and freshly ground black pepper

** Please refer to note on garlic-infused olive oil under heading 'A few specific notes about low-FODMAP cooking', page 89.*

To make the Dressing, combine all the ingredients in a bowl, adding the mustard to taste. Using a hand-held blender, blend until smooth in texture with no lumps. If necessary, press through a fine sieve. Set aside until ready to serve.

To make the Individual Caesar Salads, in a small non-stick frying pan, sauté the bacon until golden brown.

Using the same pan, heat the olive oil over a medium–high heat and add the bread. Toss the bread in the oil until golden brown on all sides. Remove from the pan and place on a plate lined with paper towel to absorb any excess oil.

Bring a saucepan of water to a gentle simmer and poach the eggs.

(**Cheat's Method of Poaching Eggs:** Line four small teacups with plastic wrap (about 15 cm square), so the wrap comes up over the edge of the teacups. Crack an egg into each teacup. Gather the edges of the wrap and twist the edges together at the top, knotting firmly to enclose the egg. Place the eggs in the saucepan and cook for 3 minutes. Remove from the pan and discard the plastic wrap.)

Divide the lettuce leaves, bacon, parmesan and croutons among four bowls. Drizzle the dressing over each salad, top with a freshly poached egg, and serve.

SERVES 4

IF YOU CAN TOLERATE

FRUCTANS, *you may substitute* ***regular bread*** *for the gluten-free bread (if you are not also gluten-free).*

MOROCCAN ROAST VEGETABLE SALAD

- 1 teaspoon finely grated orange zest
- ½ teaspoon ground cinnamon
- 1½ teaspoons ground cumin
- 1½ teaspoons ground coriander
- 1½ teaspoons ground ginger
- ½ teaspoon cayenne pepper
- ¼ teaspoon chilli powder
- a pinch of ground cloves
- salt
- ½ teaspoon freshly ground black pepper
- 300 g Jap pumpkin, cut into 3 cm cubes
- 300 g sweet potato, peeled and cut into 3 cm cubes
- 300 g small potatoes, halved
- 3 large carrots, cut into chunks
- 1 large red capsicum, cut into chunks
- 2 tablespoons garlic-infused olive oil *
- 2 tablespoons olive oil
- 3 cups baby spinach leaves
- 2 tablespoons chopped chives

** Please refer to note on garlic-infused olive oil under heading 'A few specific notes about low-FODMAP cooking', page 89.*

Preheat the oven to 200°C.

Combine the orange zest, spices, salt and pepper in a small bowl, mixing well.

Place all the vegetables, except for the spinach, into a bowl. Drizzle over the olive oils and toss to coat well. Sprinkle with the spice mix and toss to combine, ensuring an even coating.

Place the vegetables in two roasting dishes and bake for 45 minutes or until all the vegetables soften and begin to turn golden brown. Turn the vegetables twice during cooking. Remove from the oven and cover the trays with foil. Cool to room temperature.

To serve, place the spinach and roasted vegetables into a large salad bowl. Mix well to combine. Sprinkle with the chives, season to taste, and serve immediately or place in the refrigerator to cool completely before serving.

SERVES 6

IF YOU CAN TOLERATE

MANNITOL, *add whole **mushrooms** to the roasting pan after 40 minutes, so total cooking time for mushrooms is 20 minutes.*

FRUCTANS, *consider using ½ clove **garlic**, crushed and sautéed in olive oil, rather than garlic-infused olive oil.*

CHICKEN AND QUINOA SALAD

- 2 teaspoons ground cumin
- 2 teaspoons ground coriander
- 1 teaspoon ground turmeric
- 1 teaspoon sweet paprika
- 60 mL (¼ cup) garlic-infused olive oil *
- 400 g chicken tenderloins, cut into thin strips
- 2 tablespoons garlic-infused olive oil (extra) *
- 500 mL (2 cups) water
- 2 cardamom pods, crushed
- 200 g (1 cup) quinoa †
- ½ cup mint
- 2 cups baby spinach leaves
- salt and freshly ground black pepper

** Please refer to note on garlic-infused olive oil under heading 'A few specific notes about low-FODMAP cooking', page 89.*

† Use brown rice if quinoa is unavailable.

Combine the cumin, coriander, turmeric, paprika and olive oil in a small bowl. Use to coat the chicken strips, cover and marinate in the refrigerator for 2–3 hours.

When ready to cook, heat the extra oil in a medium-sized frying pan over a medium heat. Add the chicken and sauté for 4–5 minutes until cooked through. Remove from the heat and set aside.

Bring the water and cardamom pods to the boil over a medium–high heat in a small saucepan. Reduce the heat to medium and add the quinoa. Cook for 10–15 minutes or until all the water is absorbed and the quinoa is tender and cooked. Remove and discard the cardamom pods and cool the quinoa to room temperature. Toss through the chicken, mint and spinach, and season to taste.

SERVES 4

IF YOU CAN TOLERATE

FRUCTANS, *consider using ½ clove* ***garlic,*** *crushed and sautéed in olive oil, rather than garlic-infused olive oil.*

CRAB CAKES

4 × 170 g cans shredded crabmeat, very well drained, or light white-fleshed fish such as snapper

1 egg, lightly beaten

2 tablespoons finely chopped lemongrass, white part only

½ small red chilli, seeded and finely chopped

2 tablespoons finely chopped coriander leaves

4–5 green beans, topped and tailed, thinly sliced

2 tablespoons gluten-free cornflour

rice bran oil or peanut oil for frying

lime wedges, for squeezing (optional)

DIPPING SAUCE

1 tablespoon gluten-free, garlic-free sweet chilli sauce

60 mL (¼ cup) lime juice

2 tablespoons sesame oil

Combine the crabmeat, egg, lemongrass, chilli, coriander, beans and cornflour. Cover and refrigerate for 2 hours to allow the flavours to combine.

To make the Dipping Sauce, combine all the ingredients in a bowl and stir well.

Heat the rice bran oil in a large non-stick frying pan to a depth of 1 cm. Shape the crab mixture into patties of about 4 cm in diameter. Add 3–4 crab cakes at a time and cook for 1–2 minutes or until golden brown. Turn and cook the other side for 1–2 minutes. Remove from the heat and transfer to a plate lined with paper towel to absorb any excess oil.

Serve with the dipping sauce. Squeeze juice from lime wedges on top, if desired.

MAKES ABOUT 20

IF YOU CAN TOLERATE

FRUCTANS, *you may use* ***regular sweet chilli sauce*** *rather than garlic-free (if you are not also gluten-free).*

BEEF NOODLE SOUP

- 100 g dried flat rice noodles or thin mung bean (glass) noodles
- 3 cm piece ginger, thinly sliced
- 1 small red chilli, seeded and finely chopped
- 1.5 litres (6 cups) gluten-free, onion-free beef stock *
- 1½ teaspoons sesame oil
- 1½ teaspoons gluten-free soy sauce
- 150 g firm tofu, cut into 1.5 cm cubes
- 16 cherry tomatoes, halved
- 8 spears baby corn, halved lengthways
- 115 g (1 cup) bean sprouts
- 250 g porterhouse steak, sliced into very thin pieces, not more than 2 mm thick
- snowpea sprouts
- 8 fresh coriander leaves, shredded

** Please refer to note on stocks under heading 'A few specific notes about low-FODMAP cooking', page 89.*

Soak the noodles in a bowl of boiling water for 10 minutes or until softened. Drain and set aside.

Combine the ginger, chilli, stock, sesame oil and soy sauce in a large saucepan over a medium–high heat. Bring to the boil, then reduce the heat to a simmer for 10 minutes, allowing the flavours to infuse. Add the tofu, tomatoes and corn and simmer for 2–3 minutes until the tomatoes are soft. Turn the heat down to low and continue simmering.

Cover the base of each of four deep soup bowls with a handful of bean sprouts. Evenly distribute the raw beef slices, then place a handful of noodles on top.

Remove the ginger from the stock. Pour the hot soup over the beef and noodles, and stand for 3 minutes to enable the soup to cook the beef slices. Top with snowpea sprouts and coriander leaves and serve immediately.

SERVES 4

IF YOU CAN TOLERATE

MANNITOL, *add 4* ***button mushrooms****, sliced, to the stock with the ginger and chilli.*

FRUCTANS, *you may use* ***regular beef stock****, rather than onion-free (if you are not also gluten-free).*

CHICKEN AND VEGETABLE SOUP

- 2 tablespoons garlic-infused olive oil *
- 3 sprigs thyme, plus extra leaves for sprinkling
- 4 skinless chicken thigh fillets, diced
- ½ stalk celery, sliced
- 3 carrots, peeled and diced
- 1 swede, peeled and diced
- 400 g Jap pumpkin, peeled and diced
- 1 sweet potato, peeled and diced
- 1 litre (4 cups) water
- 2 litres (8 cups) gluten-free, onion-free chicken stock **
- 2 cups baby spinach leaves

** Please refer to note on garlic-infused olive oil under heading 'A few specific notes about low-FODMAP cooking', page 89.*

*** Please refer to note on stocks under heading 'A few specific notes about low-FODMAP cooking', page 89.*

Heat the olive oil in a large stockpot set over a medium heat. Add the thyme, chicken, celery and carrot. Cook until the chicken just turns golden brown and the thyme is fragrant. Add the swede, pumpkin and sweet potato to the pot, then add the water and chicken stock. Bring to the boil, then reduce the heat to medium and simmer for 25–30 minutes.

Turn off the heat, stir in the spinach to wilt, sprinkle with thyme leaves and serve.

SERVES 6

IF YOU CAN TOLERATE

MANNITOL, *add a few florets of* ***cauliflower*** *into the pot with the other vegetables.*

FRUCTANS, *consider using one of the following:* ***regular chicken stock*** *rather than onion-free (if you are not also gluten-free); or ½ clove* ***garlic****, crushed and sautéed in olive oil, rather than garlic-infused olive oil.*

ROASTED PUMPKIN AND GINGER SOUP

- 1.75 kg Jap pumpkin, peeled and cut into 2 cm pieces
- 2 tablespoons olive oil
- 1 litre (4 cups) gluten-free, onion-free chicken stock *
- 2 teaspoons grated fresh ginger
- 85 mL (1/3 cup) lactose-free cream, plus extra to serve
- salt and black pepper, freshly ground
- 2 tablespoons chopped chives

** Please refer to note on stocks under heading 'A few specific notes about low-FODMAP cooking', page 89.*

Preheat the oven to 180°C.

Place the pumpkin on a baking tray and drizzle with the olive oil. Bake for 30–40 minutes or until cooked and browned, turning occasionally.

Put the pumpkin, stock and ginger in a large stockpot and simmer over a medium–low heat, uncovered, for 15–20 minutes, stirring occasionally.

Remove from the heat and allow to cool slightly. Purée with a hand-held blender or blend in a food processor until smooth. Add the cream and continue blending until well combined. Taste, then season with salt and pepper. Garnish with the chopped chives, freshly ground salt and pepper, and a drizzle of cream, if desired.

SERVES 4

IF YOU CAN TOLERATE

LACTOSE, *you may use* ***regular*** *rather than lactose-free cream.*

FRUCTANS, *consider using one of the following:* ***regular chicken stock*** *rather than onion-free (if you are not also gluten-free); or* ***spring onions*** *rather than chives as a garnish.*

CRYING TIGER (THAI-STYLE CHARGRILLED BEEF)

- 2 tablespoons garlic-infused olive oil *
- 2 teaspoons lime juice
- 2 tablespoons chopped coriander leaves
- 2 × 200 g rib-eye steaks
- 2 tablespoons gluten-free, garlic-free sweet chilli sauce
- 3 teaspoons lime juice
- 3 teaspoons brown sugar
- 2 teaspoons fish sauce
- 200 g cherry tomatoes, halved
- 3 cups baby spinach leaves
- 5 snow peas, finely chopped
- 1 small cucumber, sliced on the diagonal
- ½–¾ cup coriander leaves (extra)
- 3 tablespoons spring onions, green part only, chopped
- 8 basil leaves

** Please refer to note on garlic-infused olive oil under heading 'A few specific notes about low-FODMAP cooking', page 89.*

In a small bowl, combine the olive oil, lime juice and coriander. Brush both sides of each steak with the oil, and place on a plate. Cover and refrigerate for 1 hour.

In a small bowl, combine the sweet chilli sauce, lime juice, brown sugar and fish sauce. Mix until well combined and allow the dressing to stand for a few minutes before using.

Cook the steaks in a hot non-stick frying pan over a medium–high heat for 3–4 minutes on each side for medium-rare or to your preference. Remove from the pan, transfer to a plate and cover with foil. Allow to rest for 5 minutes, then thinly slice.

In a large bowl, combine the tomatoes, spinach, snow peas, cucumber, extra coriander and spring onions. Drizzle the dressing over the salad and toss to coat. Divide the salad among four serving bowls. Top with the beef, scatter over the basil and serve.

SERVES 4

IF YOU CAN TOLERATE

FRUCTANS, *consider using one of the following: the* ***whole spring onion****, not just the green part; or* ***regular sweet chilli sauce*** *rather than garlic-free (if you are not also gluten-free).*

PORK TERRINE

- 1 kg pork mince
- ¼ cup chopped cornichons
- 200 g stale gluten-free low-FODMAP bread, crusts removed and crumbled
- 2 eggs, lightly whisked
- 85 mL (⅓ cup) lactose-free cream
- ½ cup chopped parsley
- ¼ cup chopped tarragon
- 60 mL (¼ cup) garlic-infused olive oil *
- 2 tablespoons butter
- 125 mL (½ cup) dry white wine
- freshly ground black pepper
- 12 thin slices prosciutto
- gluten-free low-FODMAP bread, toasted, to serve (optional)
- cherry tomatoes, roasted, to serve (optional)

** Please refer to note on garlic-infused olive oil under heading 'A few specific notes about low-FODMAP cooking', page 89.*

Preheat the oven to 180°C.

In a large bowl, combine the pork mince, cornichons, breadcrumbs, egg, cream, parsley and tarragon.

Heat the olive oil and butter over a medium heat in a small frying pan. Add the wine and heat for 1 minute. Remove from the heat.

Pour the wine mixture into the pork mixture and stir until well combined. Season with pepper (the mixture will not need salting as the prosciutto will contribute salt while cooking).

Line a 24 cm × 12 cm × 8 cm loaf tin with prosciutto, going width-ways first, then lay the remaining slices cross-ways to overhang the long sides of the tin.

Spoon the pork mixture into the lined tin and smooth the surface. Fold in the overhanging prosciutto to encase the filling. Cover the tin with foil and place in a large baking dish. Pour enough boiling water into the baking dish to submerge two-thirds of the tin.

Bake for 1 hour, or until the juices run clear when a skewer is inserted in the centre of the terrine. Set aside to cool to room temperature.

Remove the foil and turn the tin upside-down onto a wire rack over a tray to allow any juices to drain away. Turn the tin upright and re-cover with foil. Top with another loaf tin and place two or three heavy cans in the top tin to compress the terrine. Place in the refrigerator to cool completely for a few hours or overnight, to allow the flavours to develop.

To serve, turn the terrine onto a board and pat dry with paper towel. Cut into slices and serve with gluten-free, low-FODMAP toast and cherry tomatoes on the side, if desired.

SERVES 8–10

IF YOU CAN TOLERATE

MANNITOL, *add 6* **button mushrooms**, *finely chopped, to the mince mixture.*

LACTOSE, *you may use* **regular** *rather than lactose-free cream.*

FRUCTANS, *consider using 1 clove* **garlic**, *crushed and sautéed in olive oil, rather than garlic-infused olive oil. Or, you may substitute* **regular** *bread for gluten-free (if you are not also gluten-free).*

MAIN MEALS

FETTUCCINE MARINARA

- 500 g gluten-free fettuccine
- 85 mL (⅓ cup) garlic-infused olive oil *
- 250 g cherry tomatoes, chopped
- 60 mL (¼ cup) dry white wine
- 1 small red chilli, seeded and finely chopped (optional)
- 250 g raw peeled prawns
- 500 g white fish fillets, e.g. snapper, diced
- 250 g calamari tubes, cut into rings
- 4 tablespoons finely chopped chives
- 1 teaspoon finely chopped dill
- 1–2 teaspoons finely grated lemon zest
- 2–3 tablespoons lemon-infused olive oil
- salt and freshly ground black pepper

** Please refer to note on garlic-infused olive oil under heading 'A few specific notes about low-FODMAP cooking', page 89.*

Bring a large saucepan of salted water to the boil, add the fettuccine and a splash of olive oil. Cook for 8–10 minutes or until *al dente*. Drain and keep warm.

While the pasta is cooking, heat the garlic-infused olive oil in a large non-stick frying pan. Add the tomatoes, wine and chilli, if using, and cook until the tomatoes are soft. Add the prawns, fish and calamari. Toss through the tomato mixture and heat until the seafood is cooked. Add the pasta to the pan and toss through the sauce, adding the herbs, lemon zest and lemon-infused oil. Season to taste. Serve immediately.

SERVES 4

IF YOU CAN TOLERATE

FRUCTANS, *consider one of the following: use 1 clove* ***garlic****, crushed and sautéed in olive oil rather than garlic-infused olive oil; sauté* ***spring onions*** *with the cherry tomatoes; or substitute gluten-free pasta with* ***regular pasta*** *(if you can tolerate gluten).*

PASTA CARBONARA

- 3 eggs
- 200 g lean bacon, finely chopped
- 50 g (½ cup) grated parmesan
- 500 g gluten-free pasta, e.g. fettuccine
- 125 mL (½ cup) lactose-free reduced-fat cream
- 2 tablespoons finely chopped chives
- ½ cup shaved parmesan
- freshly ground black pepper

Beat the eggs. In a small frying pan, cook the bacon for 5 minutes, until soft and brown. Add the bacon and grated parmesan to the beaten eggs.

Cook the pasta in a large saucepan of salted boiling water until *al dente*.

Drain, then return to the saucepan and immediately add the cream and chives and stir through to mix well. Remove from the heat and immediately add the egg mixture, stirring, until the egg is cooked but not scrambled.

Divide among four bowls and top with the shaved parmesan and pepper.

SERVES 4

IF YOU CAN TOLERATE

LACTOSE, *use* ***regular*** *rather than lactose-free cream.*

FRUCTANS, *consider one of the following: substitute* ***spring onions*** *for chives; or substitute gluten-free pasta with* ***regular pasta*** *(if you can tolerate gluten).*

SAFFRON CHICKEN PASTA WITH SUMMER VEGETABLES

500 g gluten-free pasta, e.g. penne

2 tablespoons garlic-infused olive oil *

700 g skinless chicken tenderloins, diced

3–4 strands saffron, soaked in 1 tablespoon warm water for 15 minutes

50 g prosciutto, finely chopped

1 red capsicum, sliced into thin strips

1 zucchini, thinly sliced on the diagonal

3 cups baby spinach leaves

1 tomato, roughly chopped

3 tablespoons chopped chives

extra virgin olive oil

salt and freshly ground black pepper

50 g (½ cup) finely grated pecorino

** Please refer to note on garlic-infused olive oil under heading 'A few specific notes about low-FODMAP cooking', page 89.*

Cook the pasta in a large saucepan of salted boiling water until *al dente*. Drain.

In a large frying pan, heat the olive oil over a medium–high heat and add the chicken, saffron liquid, prosciutto and capsicum. Sauté until the chicken is golden brown and the vegetables soften. Add the zucchini, spinach, tomato and chives and toss until warmed through. Remove from the heat and toss through the pasta, adding a splash of extra virgin olive oil, and season to taste. Serve in a large bowl with the pecorino scattered over the top.

SERVES 4

IF YOU CAN TOLERATE

FRUCTANS, *consider one of the following: use 1 clove* ***garlic****, crushed and sautéed in olive oil, rather than garlic-infused olive oil; substitute* ***spring onions*** *for chives; or substitute gluten-free pasta with* ***regular pasta*** *(if you can tolerate gluten).*

SPAGHETTI BOLOGNESE

- 1 tablespoon garlic-infused olive oil *
- 200 g lean bacon, diced
- 800 g lean beef mince
- 3 thyme sprigs, plus extra to garnish (optional)
- 2 teaspoons oregano leaves, plus extra to garnish (optional)
- 700 mL (2¾ cups) tomato purée
- 2 tablespoons garlic-free tomato paste
- 125 mL (½ cup) red wine
- a splash of good-quality balsamic vinegar
- 1 bay leaf
- ½ teaspoon chilli powder (optional)
- salt and freshly ground black pepper
- 500 g gluten-free spaghetti
- shaved parmesan, to serve

** Please refer to note on garlic-infused olive oil under heading 'A few specific notes about low-FODMAP cooking', page 89.*

Heat the olive oil in a large heavy-based frying pan and sauté the bacon over medium-high heat until crisp and golden. Add the mince, thyme and oregano. Sauté until the beef is nicely browned, breaking up any lumps. Add the tomato purée and paste, wine, balsamic vinegar, bay leaf and chilli, if using. Simmer over medium heat for 20 minutes, stirring occasionally. Remove the bay leaf. Taste and season with salt and pepper.

Cook the pasta in a large saucepan of salted boiling water until *al dente*. Drain.

Toss the spaghetti through the sauce. Serve with parmesan to taste and garnish with the extra thyme or oregano leaves, if desired.

SERVES 6

IF YOU CAN TOLERATE

MANNITOL, *add 6 sliced* ***button mushrooms*** *to the frying pan with the beef, bacon and thyme.*

FRUCTANS, *consider one of the following: 1 clove* ***garlic,*** *crushed and sautéed in olive oil, rather than garlic-infused olive oil;* ***regular tomato paste,*** *not garlic-free; or* ***regular pasta*** *rather than gluten-free (if you can tolerate gluten).*

STIR-FRIED NOODLES WITH PRAWNS

- 250 g thin mung-bean (glass) noodles
- 2 tablespoons gluten-free soy sauce
- ½ small red chilli, seeded and finely chopped (optional)
- 1 teaspoon finely grated ginger
- 2 teaspoons brown sugar
- a squeeze of lime juice
- 1½ tablespoons sesame oil
- 1 tablespoon garlic-infused olive oil *
- 115 g (1 cup) bean sprouts, rinsed
- 125 g (1 cup) halved green beans
- ½ red capsicum, julienned
- 1 small carrot, peeled and julienned
- 200 g small prawns, peeled, tails intact
- 2 tablespoons mint leaves

** Please refer to note on garlic-infused olive oil under heading 'A few specific notes about low-FODMAP cooking', page 89.*

Soak the glass noodles in boiling water until soft. Drain and rinse under cold water. Set aside.

In a small bowl combine the soy sauce, chilli, if using, ginger, brown sugar and lime juice. Stir to combine, then set aside.

Heat the sesame and olive oils in a large wok over a high heat. Add the sprouts, beans, capsicum and carrot, and cook for 3–4 minutes until just soft. Add the prawns and stir-fry for 2–3 minutes until cooked through. Add the noodles and the sauce mixture. Stir through until well combined. Remove from the heat and garnish with mint leaves.

SERVES 4

IF YOU CAN TOLERATE

FRUCTANS, *you may use ½ clove* ***garlic****, crushed and sautéed in olive oil, rather than garlic-infused olive oil.*

CRISP-SKINNED SNAPPER WITH TOMATO SAUCE AND FETA SALAD

FETA SALAD

3–4 cups mixed leaves or rocket

2 tablespoons lemon-infused olive oil

2 teaspoons lemon zest strips

60 g feta, crumbled

salt and freshly ground black pepper

CRISP-SKINNED SNAPPER

1 tablespoon garlic-infused olive oil *

6 Roma tomatoes, chopped

15 cherry tomatoes, halved

¼ cup Kalamata olives in oil, drained, pitted and halved

2 tablespoons baby capers

1 tablespoon chopped chives

125 mL (½ cup) dry white wine

salt and freshly ground black pepper

4 large snapper fillets, skin on

1 tablespoon torn basil leaves

** Please refer to note on garlic-infused olive oil under heading 'A few specific notes about low-FODMAP cooking', page 89.*

To make the Feta Salad, place the salad greens in a small bowl, add the olive oil, lemon zest, feta and a few grinds of salt and pepper. Toss well to combine.

To make the Crisp-Skinned Snapper, heat the olive oil in a large frying pan. Add all the tomatoes, olives, baby capers and chives. Add the white wine, lower the heat to medium–low and simmer for 10–15 minutes until the tomatoes soften. Season to taste and keep warm over a low heat.

Add a splash of oil to a clean frying pan set over a high heat and add the snapper, skin side down. Cook, pressing the fillet into the pan to ensure all the skin is in contact with the pan. When crisp, after 4–5 minutes, turn the fillets over and spoon the tomato mixture over the skin sides, then cook. Cook over a medium heat for 2 minutes or until the snapper is done to your liking. Scatter with basil leaves and serve with the salad.

SERVES 4

IF YOU CAN TOLERATE

FRUCTANS, *consider one of the following: use ½ clove* ***garlic,*** *crushed and sautéed in olive oil, rather than garlic-infused olive oil, or substitute* ***spring onions*** *for chives.*

MUSSELS WITH WHITE WINE, LEMONGRASS AND CORIANDER

- 500 mL (2 cups) gluten-free, onion-free fish stock *
- 1 stalk lemongrass, cut into 2 cm lengths
- 375 mL (1½ cups) water
- 375 mL (1½ cups) dry white wine
- 60 mL (¼ cup) lemon juice
- 1 tablespoon finely grated lemon zest
- 1 teaspoon brown sugar
- 2 kg mussels, scrubbed and beards removed
- ½ cup coriander leaves
- salt and freshly ground black pepper

** Please refer to note on stocks under heading 'A few specific notes about low-FODMAP cooking', page 89.*

In a large heavy-based saucepan with a lid, bring the fish stock and lemongrass to the boil, then reduce the heat to medium–low to simmer for 15 minutes to infuse. Use a slotted spoon to remove the lemongrass.

Add the water, white wine, lemon juice and zest, and brown sugar to the saucepan, turn up the heat and bring the broth to the boil. Add the mussels and cover. Cook for 5–8 minutes or until most of the mussels open. Shake, then cook for an extra minute. Shake again, discarding any unopened mussels. Divide mussels and broth among serving bowls. Add the coriander, and season to taste with salt and pepper. Serve immediately.

SERVES 4

IF YOU CAN TOLERATE

FRUCTANS, *consider one of the following: add 1 finely chopped* ***spring onion*** *to the broth; or use* ***regular fish stock,*** *rather than onion-free (if you are not also gluten-free).*

TREVALLY WITH LEMONGRASS CHILLI NOODLES

- 3 tablespoons gluten-free, onion-free miso paste
- 1 tablespoon sesame oil
- 4 × 140 g trevally fillets, or whiting, salmon, snapper or other fish
- 2 tablespoons gluten-free soy sauce
- 2 tablespoons hot water
- 1 tablespoon lime juice
- 2 tablespoons finely chopped spring onion, green part only
- 2 tablespoons chopped roasted peanuts
- 2 tablespoons gluten-free, garlic-free sweet chilli sauce
- 2 tablespoons finely chopped lemongrass
- 250 g soba (100% buckwheat) noodles
- 100 g watercress

In a small bowl, combine the miso paste and sesame oil. Brush the fish with the marinade, place on a baking tray, cover with foil and refrigerate for 3–4 hours.

In a medium-sized bowl, combine the soy sauce, 2 tablespoons of hot water, lime juice, spring onion, peanuts, sweet chilli sauce and lemongrass.

Cook the noodles according to the packet instructions and drain. Set aside to cool slightly.

Toss the sauce through the noodles then cover to keep warm.

Cook the fish in a non-stick frying pan over a medium heat for 3–4 minutes. Turn and cook the other side for 2–3 minutes or to your liking.

Divide the noodles among four plates. Top with the cooked fish and garnish with the watercress.

SERVES 4

IF YOU CAN TOLERATE

FRUCTANS, *consider using one of the following: the whole* ***spring onion****, not just the green part; or* ***regular sweet chilli sauce*** *rather than garlic-free (if not also gluten-free).*

THAI-STYLE SALMON WITH COCONUT RICE

½ small red chilli, seeded and finely chopped
2 tablespoons finely chopped lemongrass
½ cup chopped coriander leaves
finely grated zest of 1 small lime
4 × 140 g Atlantic salmon fillets
salt and freshly ground black pepper

COCONUT RICE

185 mL (¾ cup) coconut cream
250 mL (1 cup) water
200 g (1 cup) jasmine rice
3 kaffir lime leaves, very finely shredded

Preheat the oven to 180°C.

To make the Coconut Rice, combine the coconut cream and water in a large saucepan. Bring to the boil over a medium-high heat then add the rice and kaffir lime leaves. Reduce the heat to medium-low and simmer, uncovered, until all the liquid is absorbed, 15–20 minutes. Stir regularly to prevent the rice from sticking to the base of the pan. Remove from the heat and fluff with a fork.

To make the Thai-Style Salmon, while the rice is cooking, in a small bowl, combine the chilli, lemongrass, coriander and lime zest until well mixed.

Distribute this mixture evenly across each salmon fillet, and spread to ensure each one is fully covered.

Place each salmon fillet on a sheet of baking paper measuring 20–25 cm square. Wrap into a parcel. Place the salmon parcels on a baking tray and bake for 12 minutes.

To serve, divide the coconut rice among four plates, unwrap the salmon fillets and place on top of the rice. Taste for seasoning.

SERVES 4

GREEN CURRY FISH

- 5 cm piece lemongrass, very thinly sliced
- 1–2 green chillies, thinly sliced
- 1 teaspoon finely grated ginger
- 20 basil leaves, chopped
- 2 tablespoons garlic-infused olive oil *
- ¼ teaspoon ground cumin
- ½ teaspoon freshly ground black pepper
- ½ teaspoon salt
- 250 mL (1 cup) gluten-free, onion-free fish stock **
- 150 g sweet potato, peeled and cut into 1 cm cubes
- 20 green beans, topped and tailed, halved
- 2 small carrots, peeled and cut into 1 cm cubes
- ½ small eggplant, cut into 1 cm cubes
- 2 small zucchini, halved lengthways and sliced
- 2 heads baby bok choy
- 700 g firm white fish fillets, e.g. snapper, John Dory, cubed
- 250–375 mL (1–1½ cups) coconut milk
- rice, to serve

** Please refer to note on garlic-infused olive oil under heading 'A few specific notes about low-FODMAP cooking', page 89.*

*** Please refer to note on stocks under heading 'A few specific notes about low-FODMAP cooking', page 89.*

Using a mortar and pestle pound the lemongrass, chillies, ginger and basil to a paste.

Heat the olive oil in a large saucepan over a medium heat. Add the paste, cumin, pepper and salt and sauté for 1–2 minutes until fragrant. Add the stock and sweet potato, green beans, carrots and eggplant. Simmer for 7–8 minutes, or until the vegetables soften.

Add the zucchini, bok choy and fish, stirring until the fish is cooked and the bok choy has wilted. Add the coconut milk. Heat through, but do not allow to boil. If more liquid is needed, add water or extra coconut milk. Serve with rice.

SERVES 4

IF YOU CAN TOLERATE

FRUCTANS, *consider using one of the following: 1 clove* ***garlic****, crushed and sautéed in olive oil, rather than garlic-infused olive oil; or* ***regular fish stock****, rather than onion-free (if you are not also gluten-free).*

MANNITOL, *consider using* ***cauliflower*** *or* ***mushrooms*** *to replace any of the vegetables listed.*

ROAST BEEF WITH FRAGRANT ASIAN FLAVOURS

- 2–3 teaspoons gluten-free cornflour
- 500 mL (2 cups) strong gluten-free, onion-free beef stock *
- 125 mL (½ cup) gluten-free soy sauce
- 2 tablespoons sesame oil
- 2 tablespoons brown sugar
- 2 teaspoons grated ginger
- 3 star anise or 2 teaspoons ground star anise
- ½ teaspoon ground cinnamon
- 1.8 kg beef sirloin roast

** Please refer to note on stocks under heading 'A few specific notes about low-FODMAP cooking', page 89.*

In a medium-sized saucepan, combine the cornflour with a little stock and mix to a smooth paste. Add the remaining stock, soy sauce, sesame oil, brown sugar, ginger, star anise and cinnamon. Stir over a medium-high heat until the mixture thickens. Remove from the heat and allow to cool to room temperature.

Place the beef in a roasting dish and pour over the marinade. Use a pastry brush to ensure the beef is well coated. Cover with foil and allow the beef to marinate in the refrigerator for 6 hours, turning the beef every 1–2 hours.

Preheat the oven to 180°C. Roast the beef, uncovered, for 30 minutes. Cover loosely with foil and cook for a further 20–30 minutes or until the juices are pale pink when pricked with a skewer. Remove from the oven, keep covered with the foil and rest for 10–15 minutes before carving into slices. Serve with steamed rice or steamed Asian greens.

SERVES 6

IF YOU CAN TOLERATE

FRUCTANS, *consider using one of the following:* ***regular beef stock****, rather than onion-free (if you are not also gluten-free); or 1 small clove* ***garlic****, crushed, added to the pot with the star anise.*

SEASONED STEAK WITH SPICY TOMATO RELISH

60 mL (¼ cup) garlic-infused olive oil *

1 tablespoon brown sugar

2 teaspoons ground turmeric

2 teaspoons smoked paprika

3 teaspoons ground coriander

4 rib-eye steaks, approx. 200g each

SPICY TOMATO RELISH

8 tomatoes, peeled and sliced

1 spring onion, green part only, very thinly sliced

1½ tablespoons salt

2 teaspoons gluten-free, dairy-free, soy-free curry powder

1¼ teaspoons mustard powder

2 teaspoons gluten-free cornflour

2 tablespoons vinegar

125 mL (½ cup) water

165 g (¾ cup) brown sugar, firmly packed

¼ teaspoon ground white pepper

¼ teaspoon ground ginger

¼ teaspoon ground nutmeg

a pinch of chilli powder (optional)

** Please refer to note on garlic-infused olive oil under heading 'A few specific notes about low-FODMAP cooking', page 89.*

To make the Spicy Tomato Relish, place the tomatoes, spring onion and salt in a medium-sized saucepan filled with boiling water. Simmer over a low heat for 15 minutes, then drain the water away, reserving the tomato mixture.

Mix the curry powder, mustard powder and cornflour in a small bowl. Add the vinegar and mix to a smooth paste.

Return the tomato mixture to the pan. Add the water to the tomato mixture and bring to the boil over a medium–high heat. Reduce the heat to medium–low and stir in the sugar and mustard paste, then simmer for 30–40 minutes or until the sauce is quite thick. Stir through the pepper, ginger, nutmeg and chilli, if using, then remove from the heat and set aside to cool. Spoon into a sterilised jar. This relish keeps for up to 7 days in the refrigerator.

To prepare the Steaks, combine the olive oil, brown sugar and spices in a bowl or jug and pour into a large plastic bag. Add the steaks and toss to coat well. Secure the bag and refrigerate for at least 3 hours.

Preheat a barbecue grill or chargrill pan to high. Grill the steaks for 2–5 minutes on each side, or until cooked to your liking. Serve with the relish.

SERVES 4

IF YOU CAN TOLERATE

FRUCTANS, *consider using one of the following: 1 clove* ***garlic,*** *crushed and sautéed in olive oil, rather than garlic-infused olive oil; or use the whole* ***spring onion****, not just the green part.*

BEEF BOURGUIGNON WITH PARSNIP CROQUETTES

- 85 mL (⅓ cup) garlic-infused olive oil *
- 2 carrots, peeled and sliced
- 1 large sprig rosemary
- 45 g (¼ cup) gluten-free cornflour
- freshly ground black pepper
- 1.2 kg lean beef, diced
- 375 mL (1½ cups) gluten-free, onion-free beef stock **
- 500 mL (2 cups) water
- 250 mL (1 cup) good red wine
- 2 tablespoons tomato paste
- 2 bay leaves
- 2 cups baby spinach leaves
- 125 g (1 cup) chopped green beans

PARSNIP CROQUETTES

- 2 medium–large parsnips, peeled and cut into small pieces
- 1 large Coliban potato, peeled and cut into small pieces
- 2 tablespoons butter
- ¼ teaspoon sweet paprika
- salt and freshly ground black pepper
- 2 eggs
- 120 g (1 cup) gluten-free breadcrumbs
- 50 g (½ cup) grated parmesan
- canola oil
- 2 tablespoons butter, extra (optional)

Heat 1 tablespoon of the olive oil in a large non-stick stockpot. Add the carrots and rosemary. Sauté until the carrot is lightly browned and softened. Remove from the pot. Set aside.

In a bowl, combine the cornflour and pepper. Dust the beef.

Heat the remaining olive oil in the stockpot. Add a third of the beef and cook, tossing, for 2–3 minutes or until golden brown. Transfer to a plate and cover with foil. Repeat with the remaining beef.

Return all the beef to the pot with the vegetables, stock, water, wine, tomato paste, rosemary and bay leaves. Stir and bring to the boil. Reduce the heat to very low and simmer, covered, stirring occasionally, for 3–4 hours or until the beef is very tender. Remove from the heat when cooked to desired tenderness.

To make the Parsnip Croquettes, cook the parsnips and potato in a large saucepan of boiling water until tender. Remove from the heat and drain. Mash well. Add the butter and paprika and season to taste. Set the mixture aside until cooled to room temperature.

In a shallow bowl, beat the eggs. In another shallow bowl, combine the breadcrumbs, parmesan and some salt and pepper. Mix well. Shape the parsnip mixture into logs about 8 cm long and 3 cm wide. Dip in the egg mixture, drain any excess and coat in the breadcrumb mixture. Place the finished croquettes on a large plate and repeat.

Heat the oil and extra butter, if using, in a large non-stick frying pan. Shallow-fry the croquettes. Turn to cook all sides until golden.

When ready to serve, stir the spinach and beans into the beef. Season with salt and pepper to taste. Let stand for 5 minutes. Serve the beef, vegetables and juices with the croquettes on the side.

SERVES 6–8

** Please refer to note on garlic-infused olive oil under heading 'A few specific notes about low-FODMAP cooking', page 89.*

*** Please refer to note on stocks under heading 'A few specific notes about low-FODMAP cooking', page 89.*

IF YOU CAN TOLERATE

FRUCTANS, *consider one of the following: substitute* **regular breadcrumbs** *for gluten-free; or use* **regular beef stock** *rather than onion-free (if you are not also gluten-free); or use 1 clove* **garlic**, *crushed and sautéed in olive oil, rather than garlic-infused olive oil.*

BRAISED BEEF CHEEKS WITH CREAMY POLENTA

- 4 beef cheeks (approx. 800 g), trimmed
- 5 tablespoons gluten-free cornflour
- 85 mL (⅓ cup) garlic-infused olive oil *
- 3 spring onions, green part only, sliced
- 250 mL (1 cup) red wine
- 500 mL (2 cups) gluten-free, onion-free beef stock **
- 250 mL (1 cup) water
- 2 sticks cinnamon
- 3 sprigs thyme
- 2 star anise
- 1 small red chilli, seeded and sliced (optional)
- 2 × 1 cm pieces ginger, peeled
- 2 teaspoons gluten-free soy sauce
- ½ teaspoon vinegar
- 1–2 teaspoons brown sugar
- salt and freshly ground black pepper
- 1 quantity Creamy Polenta (see page 178)

** Please refer to note on garlic-infused olive oil under heading 'A few specific notes about low-FODMAP cooking', page 89.*

*** Please refer to note on stocks under heading 'A few specific notes about low-FODMAP cooking', page 89.*

Preheat the oven to 160°C.

Toss the beef cheeks in the cornflour.

Heat 60 mL (¼ cup) of the olive oil in a large flameproof casserole dish and brown the beef cheeks, two at a time, over a medium heat, ensuring they are sealed on all sides. Set aside.

Add the remaining oil to the dish and sauté the spring onions. Add the wine, stock, water, cinnamon sticks, thyme, star anise, chilli, if using, and ginger. Bring to the boil and add the beef. Place a sheet of baking paper over the top of the beef and put the lid on. Place in the oven and cook for 3 hours, checking the liquid occasionally and topping up with water if the level is low, to help prevent sticking.

Prepare the Creamy Polenta according to the recipe on page 178.

In a small bowl, combine the soy sauce and vinegar, adding enough brown sugar to balance the acidity of the vinegar. Mix well.

Remove the dish from the oven. Discard the baking paper, remove the beef and set aside to rest, covered with foil. Pick out the cinnamon, ginger and star anise from the dish and discard.

Over a medium heat, stir to lift the residue off the bottom of the dish and continue reducing until the sauce thickens. Add the vinegar and soy mixture and stir through until well combined. Season with salt and pepper.

To serve, ladle the meat and braising juices over the polenta.

SERVES 4

IF YOU CAN TOLERATE

FRUCTANS, *consider using one of the following: 1 clove* ***garlic****, crushed and sautéed in olive oil, rather than garlic-infused olive oil;* ***regular beef stock****, rather than onion-free (if you are not also gluten-free); or the whole* ***spring onion****, not only the green part.*

PEPPER LAMB STIR-FRY WITH STICKY RICE

- 500 g lamb rump
- 2 tablespoons sesame oil
- 1 tablespoon garlic-infused olive oil *
- 3 teaspoons grated ginger
- 1 tablespoon gluten-, onion- and garlic-free oyster sauce
- 1 tablespoon gluten-free cornflour
- 2 teaspoons freshly ground black pepper
- ¼ teaspoon chilli powder (optional)
- 250 mL (1 cup) gluten-free, onion-free beef stock **
- 1 tablespoon sesame oil (extra)
- ½ teaspoon Chinese five-spice powder
- 1 bunch Chinese broccoli, cut into 3 cm lengths
- 2 cups green beans, trimmed
- ½ red capsicum, cut into strips
- 115 g (1 cup) bean sprouts
- sesame seeds, to garnish (optional)

STICKY RICE

210 g (1 cup) sushi rice or glutinous rice

** Please refer to note on garlic-infused olive oil under heading 'A few specific notes about low-FODMAP cooking', page 89.*

***Please refer to note on stocks under heading 'A few specific notes about low-FODMAP cooking', page 89.*

Cut the lamb into very thin strips. Combine the sesame and olive oils and ginger in a bowl. Add the lamb and toss to ensure it is well coated. Refrigerate for 2–3 hours.

To make the Sticky Rice, place the rice in a large bowl and cover with cold water. Stand for 10 minutes then drain into a colander and rinse the rice until the water runs clear.

Place the rice in a saucepan and add 1 cup (250 mL) cold water. Cover and bring to the boil, then reduce the heat to low. Simmer, covered, for 12 minutes or until the rice has absorbed all the water. Remove from the heat and leave to stand, covered, for 10 minutes.

To make the Pepper Lamb Stir-Fry, in a small bowl, combine the oyster sauce, cornflour, pepper and chilli powder, if using, to form a paste. Add the beef stock slowly, stirring well until evenly blended.

Heat the extra sesame oil in a wok over a medium–high heat, add the five-spice powder and stir for 1 minute to develop the flavour. Add the lamb and cook for 2 minutes or until lightly browned. Add the vegetables and stir-fry for 2–4 minutes or until tender.

Pour in the sauce, and heat through for 1–2 minutes or until thickened slightly and the sauce is coating all the meat and vegetables.

Serve the lamb and vegetables immediately, with rice on the side. Garnish with sesame seeds, if desired.

SERVES 4

IF YOU CAN TOLERATE

MANNITOL, *you may add 4 sliced* ***button mushrooms****. Or, you may substitute ¾ cup* ***cauliflower*** *florets for the Chinese broccoli.*

EXCESS FRUCTOSE, *you may substitute* ***sugar-snap peas*** *for the green beans.*

FRUCTANS, *consider using one of the following: ½ clove* ***garlic****, crushed and sautéed in olive oil, instead of the garlic-infused oil; or* ***regular beef stock*** *rather than onion-free (if you are not also gluten-free).*

ROAST LAMB WITH ROSEMARY POTATOES

1.5 kg rolled lamb leg roast

60 mL (¼ cup) garlic-infused olive oil *

125 mL (½ cup) dry red wine

250 mL (1 cup) gluten-free, onion-free beef stock **

salt and freshly ground black pepper

ROSEMARY POTATOES

12 small potatoes

100 g cheddar, grated

1 tablespoon butter

2 tablespoons rosemary leaves

125 mL (½ cup) lactose-free, low-fat milk

** Please refer to note on garlic-infused olive oil under heading 'A few specific notes about low-FODMAP cooking', page 89.*

*** Please refer to note on stocks under heading 'A few specific notes about low-FODMAP cooking', page 89.*

Preheat the oven to 180°C.

Place the lamb in a roasting tin and coat with the garlic-infused olive oil. Roast for 1 hour 20 minutes for medium, or until your desired doneness.

When the lamb is ready, remove from the roasting tin and transfer to a plate. Cover with foil and leave to rest for 10–15 minutes. Place the roasting tin over a medium heat, add the wine and cook for 5 minutes or until reduced by half. Add the stock and bring to the boil. Reduce the heat and simmer, stirring regularly, for 5 minutes or until the sauce starts to thicken. Remove the tin from the heat. Season with salt and pepper.

To make the Rosemary Potatoes, while the lamb is roasting, place the potatoes in a large saucepan and cover with cold water. Bring to the boil and cook for 10–12 minutes or until tender. Drain and cool, then peel and cut into cubes. Combine the potato and cheese in a large bowl and season with salt and pepper. Transfer to a medium-sized baking dish.

Place the butter and rosemary in a small frying pan over a medium heat and stir until the butter melts and is lightly golden. Pour over the potato mixture, then pour over the milk. Bake for 20–25 minutes.

Carve the lamb, and serve with the sauce and rosemary potatoes. Serve with your favourite low-FODMAP vegetables.

SERVES 8

IF YOU CAN TOLERATE

LACTOSE, *use* ***regular*** *rather than lactose-free milk and cream.*

FRUCTANS, *you may use* ***regular beef stock,*** *rather than onion-free (if you are not also gluten-free).*

MARINATED PORK RIBS WITH CREAMY MASH

- 2–3 teaspoons gluten-free cornflour
- 60 mL (¼ cup) water
- 2 tablespoons red-wine vinegar
- 1 teaspoon grated lemon zest
- 85 mL (⅓ cup) tomato purée
- 2 teaspoons sweet paprika
- 1 teaspoon ground cumin
- 2 tablespoons brown sugar
- 2 tablespoons garlic-infused olive oil *
- 2 kg pork spare ribs

CREAMY MASH

- 4 large Sebago or Coliban potatoes
- 85 mL (⅓ cup) lactose-free milk
- 2 tablespoons butter
- a pinch of salt
- freshly ground black pepper

*** Please refer to note on garlic-infused olive oil under heading 'A few specific notes about low-FODMAP cooking', page 89.*

Place the cornflour in a medium-sized bowl and combine with a little of the water to form a paste. Add the vinegar, lemon zest, tomato purée, paprika, cumin, brown sugar, olive oil and remaining water. Bring almost to the boil in a medium-sized saucepan, stirring continuously, until the sauce is thick enough to coat the back of a spoon. Remove from the heat and leave to cool to room temperature.

Brush the cooled sauce over the pork spare ribs, making sure they are well coated. Cover and refrigerate for 2–3 hours.

To make the Creamy Mash, put the potatoes in a large saucepan of cold water. Bring to the boil then boil gently for 15 minutes or until tender when pierced with a skewer. Drain and set aside for 5 minutes to cool slightly. Peel the potatoes and return to the pan. Add the remaining ingredients and mash until smooth. Season with pepper, cover and keep warm.

Remove the ribs from the refrigerator. Cook on a hot barbecue or in a frying pan over a medium-low heat for 8–10 minutes or until cooked through, turning regularly so the marinade doesn't burn.

Serve with creamy mash.

SERVES 4–6

IF YOU CAN TOLERATE

FRUCTANS, *consider using 3 cloves* **garlic**, *crushed and sautéed in olive oil, rather than garlic-infused olive oil.*

MOROCCAN LAMB WITH LEMON SPINACH

2 teaspoons ground cumin
2 teaspoons ground coriander
½ teaspoon ground ginger
1 teaspoon sweet paprika
¼ teaspoon cayenne pepper
½ teaspoon ground cinnamon
¼ teaspoon salt
4 large lamb leg steaks, approx. 180 g each
60 mL (¼ cup) garlic-infused olive oil *
1 × 425 g can crushed tomatoes
250 mL (1 cup) gluten-free, onion-free beef stock **
250 mL (1 cup) water

LEMON SPINACH

60 mL (¼ cup) lemon-infused olive oil
100 g baby spinach leaves (or baby kale leaves if desired)
salt and freshly ground black pepper

** Please refer to note on garlic-infused olive oil under heading 'A few specific notes about low-FODMAP cooking', page 89.*

*** Please refer to note on stocks under heading 'A few specific notes about low-FODMAP cooking', page 89.*

Combine all the spices in a plastic bag. Brush the lamb steaks with 1 tablespoon of the olive oil and place in the bag. Toss in the spice mix to ensure an even coating. Refrigerate for 2 hours if possible (the lamb will still be tasty if this is not done).

Heat the remaining olive oil in a large non-stick frying pan over a medium–high heat. Sear the lamb for 1–2 minutes on each side.

Add the tomatoes to the pan with the stock and water. Lower the heat and gently simmer for 30–40 minutes, covered, or until the lamb is tender and the sauce thickens. Stir occasionally and add extra water if liquid level gets low.

To make the Lemon Spinach, heat the olive oil in a saucepan, add the spinach and toss through until the spinach just wilts. Season to taste, and serve with the lamb.

SERVES 4

IF YOU CAN TOLERATE

FRUCTANS, *consider using one of the following: 1 clove* ***garlic,*** *crushed and sautéed in olive oil, rather than garlic-infused olive oil; or* ***regular beef stock,*** *rather than onion-free (if you are not also gluten-free).*

CRISP-SKIN PORK BELLY WITH SPICED PUMPKIN

- 1.5 kg boneless pork belly, skin on
- 2 teaspoons garlic-infused olive oil *
- 2 tablespoons olive oil
- 2 tablespoons thyme leaves
- 2 tablespoons freshly ground rock salt

SPICED PUMPKIN

- 400 g Jap pumpkin, peeled and cut into 3 cm cubes
- 2–3 tablespoons olive oil
- 2 teaspoons ground cumin
- salt and freshly ground black pepper
- 1 small red chilli, seeded and finely chopped
- 1 small bunch coriander leaves

** Please refer to note on garlic-infused olive oil under heading 'A few specific notes about low-FODMAP cooking', page 89.*

Preheat the oven to 220°C.

Score the pork skin: make a criss-cross pattern, about 1 cm deep, being careful not to cut into the meat.

In a small bowl, combine the olive oils, thyme and salt. Rub the mixture over the pork and place in a roasting tin. Place in the oven and cook for 20 minutes. Reduce the temperature to 170°C and roast for 1 hour 40 minutes or until the pork is cooked through and the skin is crisp. Remove from the oven and allow to rest, uncovered, for 15 minutes.

Meanwhile, to make the Spiced Pumpkin, place the pumpkin and olive oil in a bag and shake to coat. Add the cumin, salt and pepper and toss to coat. Place the pumpkin on a baking tray. Bake with the pork at 170°C for the last 30–40 minutes or until the pumpkin turns a caramel brown. Remove from the heat, and transfer to a large serving bowl. Scatter over the chilli and top with the coriander.

Slice the pork and serve with the spiced pumpkin.

SERVES 6

IF YOU CAN TOLERATE

FRUCTANS, *consider using ½ clove* **garlic**, *crushed and sautéed in olive oil, rather than garlic-infused olive oil.*

BASIL AND CHILLI CHICKEN

- 12 basil leaves
- 4 Vietnamese mint leaves
- 3 sprigs lemon thyme, leaves picked
- 12 coriander seeds
- ½ teaspoon dried chilli flakes (or to taste)
- 60 mL (¼ cup) garlic-infused olive oil *
- 1 teaspoon sesame oil
- 1 tablespoon lemon-infused olive oil
- 2 teaspoons gluten-free soy sauce
- 1 tablespoon fish sauce
- 2 large pinches of salt
- freshly ground black pepper
- 1 tablespoon lime juice
- 4 large skinless chicken breast fillets
- basil leaves, to garnish
- lime wedges, to garnish
- 2 chillies, sliced, to garnish

** Please refer to note on garlic-infused olive oil under heading 'A few specific notes about low-FODMAP cooking', page 89.*

Using a mortar and pestle, grind all the fresh herbs, the coriander seeds, chilli flakes, oils, sauces, salt, pepper and lime juice to a paste.

Score the chicken breasts by making shallow cuts about 3 cm apart on one side of each breast. Flip over and repeat on the other side.

Coat the chicken with the paste, cover and marinate in the refrigerator for up to 1 hour.

Preheat a barbecue or frying pan and cook the chicken for 8–10 minutes, turning every 2 minutes to prevent burning, until cooked. Serve with steamed rice or a salad. Garnish with basil leaves, lime wedges and sliced chillies.

SERVES 4

IF YOU CAN TOLERATE

FRUCTANS, *consider using 1 clove* **garlic**, *crushed and sautéed in olive oil, rather than garlic-infused olive oil.*

CHICKEN, CHILLI AND COCONUT SALAD

- 20 g coconut flakes
- 2 teaspoons sesame oil
- 3 large skinless chicken breast fillets
- 2 teaspoons garlic-infused olive oil *
- ½ large red capsicum, cut into strips
- ½ large green capsicum, cut into strips
- ½ large yellow capsicum, cut into strips
- ¼ cup chopped coriander leaves
- 2 tablespoons chopped mint
- 4 tablespoons gluten-free, garlic-free sweet chilli sauce

** Please refer to note on garlic-infused olive oil under heading 'A few specific notes about low-FODMAP cooking', page 89.*

Soak the coconut in a bowl of very hot water for 15 minutes or until soft. Drain. Toss in the sesame oil. Set aside.

Put the chicken in a small, deep frying pan and add enough water to cover. Poach for 5 minutes, then turn the chicken and poach for a further 5 minutes or until cooked through. Drain the water and allow the chicken to cool.

When cold, shred the chicken into 2–3 cm long pieces with your hands. Set aside.

Heat the olive oil in a large frying pan over a medium–low heat. Add the capsicum and sauté for 5 minutes or until just softened. Remove from heat. In a salad bowl, combine the chicken, cooked capsicum, coconut, coriander, mint and sweet chilli sauce. Toss well to combine. Transfer to a bowl, refrigerate for 2 hours and serve cold.

SERVES 6

IF YOU CAN TOLERATE

FRUCTANS, *consider using one of the following: ½ clove* ***garlic****, crushed and sautéed in olive oil, rather than garlic-infused olive oil; or* ***regular sweet chilli sauce*** *rather than garlic-free (if not also gluten-free).*

CHICKEN PARMIGIANA

- 90 g (½ cup) gluten-free cornflour
- 2 eggs, lightly beaten
- 180 g (1½ cups) gluten-free breadcrumbs
- salt and freshly ground black pepper
- 4 skinless chicken breast fillets
- 3–4 tablespoons light olive oil
- 1 x 420 g can crushed tomatoes
- 2 tablespoons chopped parsley
- 1 teaspoon chopped oregano
- 100 g (1 cup) grated parmesan

Preheat the oven to 180°C.

Set out three shallow bowls. Put the cornflour into one, eggs into another, and breadcrumbs, salt and pepper into the last. Coat one chicken fillet in the cornflour, then dip in the egg, and then coat well in the breadcrumbs. Repeat for remaining fillets.

Heat the olive oil in a frying pan over a medium–low heat. Cook the chicken for 3–4 minutes on each side or until golden brown.

In a small frying pan, heat the tomatoes, parsley and oregano. Cook slowly, stirring occasionally, for 15 minutes.

Place the chicken on a baking tray. Top with the tomato sauce and parmesan. Cover with foil and bake for 15 minutes.

SERVES 4

IF YOU CAN TOLERATE

FRUCTANS, *consider using* ***regular breadcrumbs*** *instead of gluten-free breadcrumbs (if you are not also gluten-free).*

CHICKEN MASALA

- 85 mL (⅓ cup) garlic-infused olive oil *
- 3 tablespoons almond meal
- 2 teaspoons grated ginger
- 1½ teaspoons paprika
- 1 teaspoon ground coriander
- 1 teaspoon ground turmeric
- ½ teaspoon ground cinnamon
- 1 teaspoon ground cumin
- ½ teaspoon chilli powder
- ½ teaspoon garam masala
- 1 kg skinless chicken thigh fillets, cut into 2 cm cubes
- 185 g (⅔ cup) regular or coconut yoghurt, plus extra to serve (optional)
- 125 g (½ cup) lactose-free sour cream
- coriander leaves, to garnish
- steamed rice, to serve

** Please refer to note on garlic-infused olive oil under heading 'A few specific notes about low-FODMAP cooking', page 89.*

Heat the olive oil in a large heavy-based saucepan or stockpot over a medium–high heat. Add the ground almond meal, ginger and all the spices and stir for 30–60 seconds until fragrant. Add the chicken and toss to coat in the spices. Cook, stirring, for 4–5 minutes or until browned on all sides.

Lower the heat and cook for a further 5 minutes. Add half the yoghurt and half the sour cream, then cover and simmer gently for 1 hour or until the chicken is tender, stirring regularly to prevent sticking. Add the remaining yoghurt and sour cream and stir until heated through. Garnish with coriander leaves, a dollop of yoghurt, if desired, and serve with steamed rice.

SERVES 6

IF YOU CAN TOLERATE

LACTOSE, *use **regular** rather than lactose-free sour cream.*

FRUCTANS, *consider using 3 cloves **garlic**, crushed and sautéed in olive oil, rather than garlic-infused olive oil.*

CHICKEN TAGINE

4 tablespoons gluten-free cornflour

1 kg skinless chicken thigh fillets, cut into 2 cm cubes

2 tablespoons garlic-infused olive oil *

1 tablespoon paprika

2 teaspoons ground cumin

1 tablespoon ground ginger

1 tablespoon turmeric

¼–½ teaspoon chilli flakes (optional)

1 litre (4 cups) gluten-free, onion-free chicken stock **

2 bay leaves

1 stick cinnamon, broken in half

2 carrots, peeled and diced

2 zucchini, halved lengthways and sliced

½ cup coriander leaves, chopped

salt and freshly ground black pepper

CREAMY POLENTA

500 mL (2 cups) lactose-free milk

95 g (½ cup) instant polenta

freshly ground black pepper

** Please refer to note on garlic-infused olive oil under heading 'A few specific notes about low-FODMAP cooking', page 89.*

*** Please refer to note on stocks under heading 'A few specific notes about low-FODMAP cooking', page 89.*

Combine the cornflour and chicken in a large bowl and toss to coat well.

Heat the olive oil in a large heavy-based non-stick saucepan and add the paprika, cumin, ginger, turmeric and chilli flakes, if using. Mix well and sauté for 1 minute to develop the flavours.

Add the chicken and cook for 4–5 minutes until browned on all sides. Add the stock, bay leaves and cinnamon sticks. Bring to the boil, then lower the heat, cover and simmer gently for 1½ hours.

Add the carrots and zucchini and simmer, uncovered, for a further 10–20 minutes, stirring occasionally, until the vegetables are tender.

To make the Creamy Polenta, heat the milk in a medium-sized saucepan until almost boiling. Add the polenta and stir until the mixture boils. Lower the heat and cook, stirring constantly, for a further 3–5 minutes until the polenta is cooked (it should be the texture of smooth mashed potato).

When ready to serve, remove the cinnamon sticks and bay leaves from the chicken tagine. Stir through the coriander and season with salt and pepper. Serve with the creamy polenta.

SERVES 6–8

IF YOU CAN TOLERATE

LACTOSE, *use **regular** rather than lactose-free milk.*

FRUCTANS, *consider using one of the following: 1 clove **garlic,** crushed and sautéed in olive oil, rather than garlic-infused olive oil; or **regular chicken stock,** rather than onion-free (if you are not also gluten-free).*

CRUMBED CHICKEN WITH SESAME GREENS

- 60 g (⅓ cup) gluten-free cornflour
- 1 teaspoon ground paprika
- 1 teaspoon grated lemon zest
- 2 eggs, lightly beaten
- 240 g (2 cups) gluten-free breadcrumbs
- salt and freshly ground black pepper
- 4 large skinless chicken breasts, halved lengthways
- 85 mL (⅓ cup) canola oil
- 2 tablespoons butter

SESAME GREENS

- 1½ tablespoons sesame oil
- 1 tablespoon sesame seeds
- 6 cups Asian greens, e.g. bok choy, choi sum, gai laan, cut into 3 cm pieces

Set out three shallow bowls. Put the cornflour into one with the paprika and lemon zest. Place the eggs in another, and the breadcrumbs, salt and pepper into the last.

Coat the chicken first in the cornflour, then dip in the egg, and finally coat well in the breadcrumbs. Repeat with the other fillets.

Heat the canola oil and butter in a frying pan over a medium-low heat. Cook the chicken in batches for 3–5 minutes on each side or until golden brown.

To make the Sesame Greens, heat the sesame oil in a hot wok, add the sesame seeds and vegetables and toss well to combine. Cook until vegetables are just tender, 2–3 minutes.

Serve the chicken, sliced, with the greens.

SERVES 4

IF YOU CAN TOLERATE

FRUCTANS, *consider using* ***regular breadcrumbs*** *instead of gluten-free breadcrumbs (if you are not also gluten-free).*

VEGETARIAN

FOUR CHEESE RISOTTO

- 1.25 litres (5 cups) gluten-free, onion-free vegetable stock † * ‡
- 2 tablespoons garlic-infused olive oil, plus extra to serve **
- 330 g (1½ cups) arborio rice
- 250 mL (1 cup) dry white wine
- 1½ tablespoons gorgonzola (adjust according to taste)
- 1½ tablespoons grated parmesan, plus extra to serve
- 1½ tablespoons grated taleggio or Swiss cheese
- 1½ tablespoons mascarpone
- 1 tablespoon butter
- salt and freshly ground black pepper
- 3 tablespoons finely chopped chives

† This will make a thick risotto; if you prefer it thinner, add more stock.

** Please refer to note on stocks under heading 'A few specific notes about low-FODMAP cooking', page 89.*

‡ If you cannot find onion-free vegetable stock, onion-free chicken stock may be used instead – however, dish will no longer be vegetarian.

*** Please refer to note on garlic-infused olive oil under heading 'A few specific notes about low-FODMAP cooking', page 89.*

Heat the stock in a medium-sized saucepan over a low heat and keep covered at a low simmer so the stock is kept warm but does not evaporate.

Heat the olive oil in a large saucepan over a medium heat. Add the rice to the pan and stir until the rice is well coated. Add the wine and stir until it is fully absorbed.

Add 125 mL (½ cup) hot stock, stirring, until it has been completely absorbed. Repeat this process, adding ½ cup stock at a time, until all the stock has been used and the rice is *al dente*. This will take about 20 minutes. Turn off the heat, then stir through the cheeses and butter. Season to taste. Rest, covered, for 5 minutes. Spoon into serving bowls. Drizzle with extra olive oil, then sprinkle with extra parmesan cheese and the chives.

SERVES 4–6

IF YOU CAN TOLERATE

FRUCTANS, *consider using one of the following: 1 clove* ***garlic****, crushed and sautéed in olive oil, rather than garlic-infused olive oil; or* ***regular vegetable stock*** *rather than onion-free stock (if you are not also gluten-free).*

TOMATO, BASIL AND MOZZARELLA ARANCINI

- 440 g (2 cups) medium-grain white rice
- 2 eggs, lightly beaten
- 100 g (1 cup) grated parmesan
- 1 tablespoon basil leaves, finely chopped
- 125 g cherry tomatoes, chopped
- salt and freshly ground black pepper
- 100 g mozzarella, cut into cubes
- 120 g (⅔ cup) gluten-free cornflour
- 2 eggs, lightly beaten, extra
- 180 g (1½ cups) gluten-free breadcrumbs
- vegetable oil, for frying
- whole-egg mayonnaise, for serving

Preheat the oven to 150°C.

Cook the rice in a large saucepan of boiling water for 10–12 minutes or until tender, stirring occasionally. Remove from the heat, drain and allow to cool to room temperature.

Place the cooled rice, eggs, parmesan, basil and cherry tomatoes in a large bowl and mix well. Season to taste.

Roll the rice into balls, a little larger than a golfball in size, fully encasing a piece of mozzarella in the middle of each ball. Chill for at least 1 hour.

Set out three shallow bowls: put the cornflour in one, the beaten egg in another, and the breadcrumbs in the last bowl. Roll the balls in the cornflour to lightly coat, dip them in the egg, then toss in the breadcrumbs (make sure they are well coated).

Fill a large saucepan with enough vegetable oil to cover the arancini and heat over a medium–high heat (the oil is hot enough when a cube of bread dropped into it browns in 10 seconds). Cook 3–4 balls at a time for 3–4 minutes or until golden brown. Remove with a slotted spoon and drain on paper towel. Transfer to a baking tray and keep warm in the oven while you cook the rest of the arancini. Serve with whole-egg mayonnaise.

SERVES 6–8

IF YOU CAN TOLERATE

FRUCTANS, *consider using* **regular breadcrumbs** *instead of gluten-free breadcrumbs (if you are not also gluten-free).*

PAN-FRIED GNOCCHI WITH ROASTED CAPSICUM SAUCE

- 1 kg Desirée potatoes, cut into 2 cm pieces
- salt and freshly ground black pepper
- 1 tablespoon chopped flat-leaf parsley
- 1½ tablespoons chopped basil
- 1½ tablespoons chopped chives
- 1 tablespoon garlic-infused olive oil *
- 180 g (1 cup) potato flour
- 90 g (½ cup) gluten-free cornflour, plus extra for dusting
- 1 egg yolk, lightly whisked
- grated parmesan
- basil leaves, to garnish

ROASTED CAPSICUM SAUCE

- 3 red capsicums, quartered
- 2 tablespoons garlic-infused olive oil
- 1 tablespoon extra virgin olive oil
- 2 sprigs thyme
- ¼–½ teaspoon chilli powder (optional)
- 1–2 teaspoons balsamic vinegar
- 125 mL (½ cup) water
- 1 x 420 g can diced tomatoes
- salt and freshly ground black pepper

** Please refer to note on garlic-infused olive oil under heading 'A few specific notes about low-FODMAP cooking', page 89.*

To make the Roasted Capsicum Sauce, preheat the oven to 180°C. Place the capsicums on a baking tray, skin side up, and bake for 20 minutes or until the skins blacken and blister. Alternatively, grill on high heat for 5–8 minutes to achieve the same effect. Remove from the heat, and place into a plastic bag. Seal and leave to sit for 10 minutes. Remove from the bag and the skins should peel off easily. Discard the skins and roughly chop the capsicum flesh.

Place the capsicum in a large non-stick frying pan and add the olive oils, thyme, chilli, if using, balsamic vinegar, water and tomatoes. Simmer over a medium heat for 10–15 minutes until the flavours develop well and the sauce reduces. Season to taste.

To make the Gnocchi, cook the potato in a saucepan of boiling water until tender. Drain and transfer to a large heatproof bowl. Mash until smooth, then season well with salt and pepper. Stir in the herbs and olive oil.

Sift the flours into a small bowl and mix well with a wooden spoon. Add 3 tablespoons of the flour mixture and the egg yolk to the mashed potato and stir until combined. Stir in the remaining flour in 2 batches, then gently form into a soft dough. Place the dough on a benchtop dusted with cornflour and knead lightly.

Divide the dough into six equal portions. Roll one portion into a log about 30 cm long and 1 cm wide, then cut into 2 cm lengths. Repeat with the remaining dough.

Bring a large saucepan of water to the boil over a high heat. Add the gnocchi in small batches and cook for 3–4 minutes or until they float to the surface. Remove with a slotted spoon and place in a large bowl. Bring the water back to the boil between each batch.

Toss the cooked gnocchi through the sauce and serve. Garnish with basil leaves. Top with parmesan if desired.

SERVES 6

IF YOU CAN TOLERATE

MANNITOL, *you may add 4* **button mushrooms**, *sliced, with the diced tomatoes to the frying pan for the capsicum sauce.*

FRUCTANS, *consider using one of the following: 1 clove* **garlic**, *crushed and sautéed in olive oil, rather than garlic-infused olive oil. Or, replace the cornflour with plain wheat flour (if you are not also gluten-free).*

ASIAN OMELETTE

2 teaspoons garlic-infused olive oil *

50 g baby corn spears, halved lengthways

1 baby bok choy, leaves separated

4 eggs

50 g (½ cup) grated cheddar

½ small red chilli, seeded and chopped

2 teaspoons chopped coriander leaves

1 teaspoon chopped lemongrass

salt and freshly ground black pepper

1 tablespoon sesame oil

** Please refer to note on garlic-infused olive oil under heading 'A few specific notes about low-FODMAP cooking', page 89.*

Heat the olive oil in a non-stick frying pan, then add the corn and bok choy. Sauté until the bok choy wilts and the corn changes colour. Remove from the heat and set aside, keeping warm.

Whisk together the eggs, cheddar, chilli, coriander, lemongrass, salt and pepper.

Heat the sesame oil in a small frying pan over a medium heat. Add half of the mixture to the pan and cook until almost set on top. Carefully lift at the edges with an egg slide, and shake the omelette loose.

Place half of the corn and bok choy over half of the omelette, then fold over to encase – the omelette will be warm enough to finish cooking the top side. Transfer to a plate and keep warm by covering with foil while cooking the second omelette.

SERVES 2

IF YOU CAN TOLERATE

MANNITOL, *you may add 2* ***button mushrooms****, sliced, with the corn spears and bok choy to the frying pan.*

FRUCTANS, *consider using 1 clove* ***garlic****, crushed and sautéed in olive oil, rather than garlic-infused olive oil.*

STIR-FRIED SOBA NOODLES

- 200 g soba (100% buckwheat) noodles
- 2 teaspoons sesame oil
- 3 teaspoons garlic-infused olive oil *
- 3 tablespoons thinly sliced ginger
- 1 tablespoon finely chopped kaffir lime leaves
- 35 g (¼ cup) roasted peanuts
- 1 carrot, peeled and julienned
- 150 g green beans, thinly sliced on the diagonal
- 1 red capsicum, thinly sliced
- 75 g (½ cup) sliced bamboo shoots
- 115 g (1 cup) bean sprouts
- 3 teaspoons gluten-free cornflour
- 1 tablespoon gluten-free soy sauce
- 3 tablespoons crunchy peanut butter
- 375 mL (1½ cups) water
- 150 g firm tofu, cut into 2 cm cubes

** Please refer to note on garlic-infused olive oil under heading 'A few specific notes about low-FODMAP cooking', page 89.*

Cook the noodles in a saucepan of boiling water according to the packet instructions. Drain and rinse well under hot water. Transfer to a heatproof bowl and splash a little of the sesame oil over the noodles to coat. Cover with foil to keep warm, and set aside.

In a wok, heat the remaining sesame oil and the olive oil until just smoking. Lower the heat and add the ginger, lime leaves and peanuts and stir-fry for 2–3 minutes until fragrant. Add all the vegetables and stir-fry for 3–5 minutes or until tender.

In a small bowl, combine the cornflour with the soy sauce and peanut butter to form a paste. Stir in the water.

Pour into the wok and stir through. Add the tofu, and stir-fry until the sauce thickens. Finally add the noodles, and stir well. Serve immediately.

SERVES 4

IF YOU CAN TOLERATE

MANNITOL, *consider adding sliced* ***shiitake mushrooms*** *or* ***cauliflower florets*** *with the other vegetables.*

EXCESS FRUCTOSE, *substitute* ***sugar-snap peas*** *for the green beans.*

GOAT'S CHEESE AND SWEET POTATO FRITTATA

- 280 g sweet potato, cut into 2 cm cubes
- 8 eggs, lightly beaten
- 1 × 160 g can gluten-free creamed corn
- 1 tablespoon garlic-infused olive oil *
- 1 spring onion, green part only, thinly sliced
- 1 teaspoon thyme leaves
- salt and freshly ground black pepper
- 125 g goat's cheese, crumbled

** Please refer to note on garlic-infused olive oil under heading 'A few specific notes about low-FODMAP cooking', page 89.*

Preheat the oven to 170°C. Grease a deep 16 cm round ovenproof baking dish.

Blanch the sweet potato in boiling water for 4–5 minutes, without over cooking, then drain.

Combine the eggs, corn, olive oil, spring onion, thyme, salt and pepper in a large bowl and mix together well.

Arrange alternate layers of sweet potato and goat's cheese in the baking dish, then pour the egg mixture over the top. Gently tap the baking dish on the benchtop to ensure the egg mixture is evenly distributed and fills all the gaps. Bake for 25–30 minutes or until golden brown. Leave for 5 minutes before serving. This may be served cold or at room temperature.

Serve with a salad drizzled with olive oil and balsamic vinegar.

SERVES 4–6

IF YOU CAN TOLERATE

FRUCTANS, *you may use the whole* **spring onion**, *not only the green part.*

PASTA PUTTANESCA

- 2 tablespoons garlic-infused olive oil *
- 1 tablespoon capers in salt
- 75 g black olives, pitted and chopped
- 1 × 420 g can chopped tomatoes
- 60 mL (¼ cup) white wine
- 2 tablespoons chopped basil
- 2 tablespoons chopped parsley
- salt and freshly ground black pepper
- 500 g gluten-free pasta

** Please refer to note on garlic-infused olive oil under heading 'A few specific notes about low-FODMAP cooking', page 89.*

Heat the olive oil in a large frying pan over a medium heat. Add the capers and olives and sauté for 2–3 minutes to develop the flavours. Add the tomatoes and wine, lower the heat and simmer for 15 minutes. Stir through the basil and parsley and season to taste. Set aside, keeping warm.

Cook the pasta in a large saucepan of boiling water until *al dente*. Drain.

Add the pasta to the frying pan and toss through the sauce. Serve immediately.

SERVES 4

IF YOU CAN TOLERATE

FRUCTANS, *consider using one of the following: 1 clove* ***garlic,*** *crushed and sautéed in olive oil, rather than garlic-infused olive oil; or* ***regular pasta*** *rather than gluten-free (if you are not also gluten-free).*

GOS *and* FRUCTANS, *consider adding 1 cup of canned* ***chickpeas,*** *drained, to the sauce.*

QUINOA WITH CAPSICUM, BASIL AND LEMON

2 teaspoons brown mustard seeds

1½ tablespoons ground coriander

2 pinches of saffron

2 tablespoons olive oil

300 g (1½ cups) quinoa

750 mL (3 cups) gluten-free, onion-free vegetable stock * †

2 teaspoons garlic-infused olive oil **

1 red capsicum, diced

⅓ cup chopped basil

1 spring onion, green part only, thinly sliced

2 tablespoons grated lemon zest

100 g feta, crumbled (optional)

salt and freshly ground black pepper

** Please refer to note on stocks under heading 'A few specific notes about low-FODMAP cooking', page 89.*

† If you cannot find onion-free vegetable stock, onion-free chicken stock may be used instead – however, dish will no longer be vegetarian.

*** Please refer to note on garlic-infused olive oil under heading 'A few specific notes about low-FODMAP cooking', page 89.*

Toast the mustard seeds, coriander and saffron in the olive oil in a large saucepan until fragrant, 1–2 minutes. Add the quinoa and stir until well coated. Turn up the heat, add the vegetable stock and bring to the boil. Lower the heat and cook, covered, stirring occasionally, for 25–30 minutes or until all the liquid is absorbed. Remove from the heat.

Heat the garlic-infused olive oil over a medium heat in a medium-sized non-stick frying pan and add the capsicum. Cook until it softens.

Stir the capsicum through the quinoa with the basil, spring onion and lemon zest. Sprinkle with feta (if using) and season to taste with salt and pepper.

SERVES 4

IF YOU CAN TOLERATE

FRUCTANS, *consider using one of the following: 1 clove* ***garlic****, crushed and sautéed in olive oil, rather than garlic-infused olive oil; or* ***regular vegetable stock****, rather than onion-free (if you are not also gluten-free); or the whole* ***spring onion****, not only the green part.*

KIDS

MEATBALLS WITH PASTA

4–5 slices gluten-free low-FODMAP bread, crusts removed

125 mL (½ cup) lactose-free milk

200 g lean pork or veal mince

380 g lean beef mince

1 egg, beaten

2 teaspoons garlic-infused olive oil, plus extra for cooking *

2 tablespoons finely chopped spring onion, green part only

2 tablespoons chopped basil

3 tablespoons chopped parsley

¼ teaspoon cayenne pepper

freshly ground black pepper

oil for frying

375 mL (1½ cups) tomato purée

1 tablespoon thyme leaves

500 g gluten-free pasta, e.g. penne

grated parmesan (optional)

** Please refer to note on garlic-infused olive oil under heading 'A few specific notes about low-FODMAP cooking', page 89.*

Place the bread in a shallow bowl. Cover with the milk and leave to soak for 5 minutes. Squeeze the milk from the bread and crumble. Set aside. Discard the milk.

Combine the minces, breadcrumbs, egg, olive oil, spring onion, basil, parsley, cayenne pepper and black pepper in a large mixing bowl. Shape into golfball-sized balls.

Heat a little extra oil in a large non-stick frying pan, add the meatballs and cook until browned and cooked through. Add the tomato purée and thyme, stirring to mix well. Allow the mixture to cook down slightly.

Cook the pasta in boiling water until *al dente*. Drain.

Serve the meatballs with the pasta. Top with parmesan if desired.

SERVES 6–8

IF YOU CAN TOLERATE

LACTOSE, *use* ***regular*** *rather than lactose-free milk.*

FRUCTANS, *consider using one of the following: ½ clove* ***garlic****, crushed and sautéed in olive oil, rather than garlic-infused olive oil;* ***regular bread or pasta*** *for gluten-free (if you are not also gluten-free); or the whole* ***spring onion****, not just the green part.*

3 IN 1
LIGHTNING SHREDDER
PAT. PEND.

CHICKEN DRUMSTICKS

- 2 teaspoons gluten-free cornflour
- 60 mL (¼ cup) gluten-free soy sauce
- 2 tablespoons brown sugar
- ¼ teaspoon Chinese five-spice powder
- 1 tablespoon garlic-infused olive oil *
- 2 tablespoons sesame oil
- 8 x chicken drumsticks
- sesame seeds

** Please refer to note on garlic-infused olive oil under heading 'A few specific notes about low-FODMAP cooking', page 89.*

In a small saucepan, combine the cornflour with a little of the soy sauce to make a smooth paste. Add the remaining soy sauce, and the brown sugar, five-spice powder, olive oil and sesame oil.

Heat over a medium–high heat until the sauce thickens. Remove from the heat and cool to room temperature.

Place the chicken in a large baking dish and pour over the marinade. Brush each drumstick to ensure it is well coated. Cover and refrigerate for a few hours.

Preheat the grill or a barbecue plate to medium–high. Cook the drumsticks, turning occasionally, until all the juices run clear when the drumsticks are pierced in the thickest part with a skewer. Sprinkle sesame seeds over drumsticks. Alternatively, the chicken drumsticks can be baked in a preheated 180°C oven for 15–20 minutes.

SERVES 4–8

IF YOU CAN TOLERATE

FRUCTANS, *consider using 1 clove* ***garlic****, crushed and sautéed in olive oil, rather than garlic-infused olive oil.*

FISH IN BATTER

- 70 g (½ cup) fine rice flour
- 180 g (1 cup) gluten-free cornflour
- 1 teaspoon salt
- freshly ground black pepper
- 250 mL (1 cup) cold water
- sunflower or rice bran oil
- 600 g white fish fillets, e.g. flathead or ling
- 3 tablespoons extra gluten-free cornflour, for dusting
- salt, to season
- 2 lemons, cut into wedges

Put the flours, salt and some pepper in a large bowl. Use a whisk to combine well. Make a well in the centre and slowly pour in the cold water, whisking to form a smooth batter.

Half-fill a deep-fryer or large heavy-based saucepan with sunflower oil and heat to 190°C – the oil is hot enough when a cube of bread thrown into the oil browns in 15 seconds.

Dust the fish fillets in the extra cornflour, then dip them in the batter, one at a time, allowing any excess batter to drain off. Holding the tail end, gently lower the fish into the oil; when the head end rises to the surface, let go of the fillet. This will prevent the fish from sticking to the side of the pan. Cook the fish in batches for 3–4 minutes or until golden brown and crisp. Drain on paper towel.

Season the fish with salt and serve with lemon wedges on the side. Serve with hot chips (gluten-free if needed).

SERVES 4–6

IF YOU CAN TOLERATE

FRUCTANS, *consider using ½ cup plain wheat flour instead of fine rice flour (if you are not also gluten-free).*

OMELETTE WRAPS

200 g cooked chicken breast, roughly chopped
3–4 teaspoons whole-egg mayonnaise
salt and freshly ground black pepper
cooking oil spray
6 eggs
1 small ripe avocado, peeled, stoned and cut into slices
2 medium tomatoes, sliced
½ cup shredded lettuce leaves
80 g (½ cup) grated carrot

In a small bowl, combine the chicken and mayonnaise and mix until well combined. Season with salt and pepper to taste.

Set a medium-sized non-stick frying pan over a medium heat and spray with cooking oil spray. Crack an egg into a small bowl and whisk with a fork. Pour into the frying pan, tilting the pan to ensure the egg is spread thinly and evenly over the pan, to about 12 cm in diameter. Cook for 30–60 seconds, then flip, taking care not to break the omelette. Transfer to a plate and repeat with the remaining eggs. (Alternatively, if you have a flat sandwich press, cook the omelette in that.)

Place the omelette on a benchtop. Spread 2–3 tablespoons of the chicken mixture on the top half of each omelette, and top with a few slices of avocado and the vegetables. Fold the bottom third of the omelette base up into the centre of the omelette. Roll from left to right, encasing all contents in the wrap.

Serve immediately or cover and refrigerate.

MAKES 6

IF YOU CAN TOLERATE

MANNITOL, *you may also use* ***mushrooms*** *in the filling.*

MEATLOAF

800 g lean beef mince
80 g (⅔ cup) dried gluten-free breadcrumbs
1 spring onion, green part only, chopped
150 g lean bacon rashers, chopped
1 tablespoon garlic-infused olive oil *
2 small zucchini, grated
185 mL (¾ cup) lactose-free milk
¼ teaspoon ground nutmeg
¼ teaspoon cayenne pepper
1 egg
salt and freshly ground black pepper

** Please refer to note on garlic-infused olive oil under heading 'A few specific notes about low-FODMAP cooking', page 89.*

Preheat the oven to 180°C. Grease a 23 cm × 13 cm × 7 cm loaf tin.

Combine all the ingredients in a large bowl, then press into the loaf tin and bake for 50–60 minutes or until firm to the touch and cooked through. Remove from the oven, cover with foil and leave to rest for 10–15 minutes.

To serve, invert the meatloaf onto a chopping board and cut into 2 cm thick slices. Serve hot or cold.

SERVES 8

IF YOU CAN TOLERATE

LACTOSE, *use* ***regular*** *rather than lactose-free milk.*

FRUCTANS, *consider one of the following: substitute* ***regular breadcrumbs*** *for gluten-free breadcrumbs (if you are not also gluten-free); use the whole* ***spring onion****, not only the green part.*

LUNCHBOX IDEAS

- Omelette Wraps (see page 205)
- Rice paper rolls with low-FODMAP fillings
- Sushi
- Tomato, Basil and Mozzarella Arancini (see page 186)
- Chicken Drumsticks (see page 203)
- Fritters using low-FODMAP vegetables and/or leftover meats
- Goat Cheese and Sweet Potato Frittata (see page 192)
- Corn chips and yoghurt/cucumber dip
- Savoury muffins
- Boiled eggs
- Low-FODMAP fruit (see page 26)
- Low-FODMAP vegetable sticks (see page 26)
- Rice cakes/corn thins with cheese and cold meats
- Cold or toasted sandwiches made from gluten-free, low-FODMAP bread with low-FODMAP fillings
- Plain popcorn
- Yoghurt lactose-free if needed
- Salads (low-FODMAP vegetables) and cold unprocessed meats, chicken or eggs
- Leftovers from last night's low-FODMAP dinner

CHICKEN FRIED RICE

- 400 g (2 cups) long grain rice
- 2 tablespoons light olive oil
- 1½ teaspoons Chinese five-spice powder
- ½ teaspoon ground cumin
- 1 tablespoon grated ginger
- 2 teaspoons garlic-infused olive oil *
- 500 g skinless chicken breast fillets, sliced
- 1 carrot, peeled and julienned
- 10 snow peas, trimmed and sliced
- 1 small red capsicum, julienned
- ½ green capsicum, julienned
- 1 × 225 g can bamboo shoots, drained
- 115 g (1 cup) bean sprouts
- salt and freshly ground black pepper

** Please refer to note on garlic-infused olive oil under heading 'A few specific notes about low-FODMAP cooking', page 89.*

In a large saucepan, bring 1 litre (4 cups) of water to the boil. Add the rice and cook for 13–15 minutes until absorbed.

Meanwhile, heat 1 tablespoon of the light olive oil in a large wok or frying pan over a medium heat. Add the five-spice powder, cumin, ginger and olive oil and cook until fragrant. Add the chicken and toss for a few minutes until just browned. Add the carrot, snow peas, capsicum, bamboo shoots and bean sprouts and cook until the vegetables are tender.

Add the rice and stir until well combined. Finally, add the rest of the light olive oil and season to taste with salt and pepper.

SERVES 6–8

IF YOU CAN TOLERATE

EXCESS FRUCTOSE, *you may substitute* **sugar-snap peas** *for the green capsicum.*

FRUCTANS, *consider using 1 clove* **garlic**, *crushed and sautéed in olive oil, rather than garlic-infused olive oil.*

BEEF AND VEGETABLE SKEWERS

125 mL (½ cup) gluten-free soy sauce

2 tablespoons sesame oil

1 teaspoon grated ginger

300 g beef steak, e.g. rump or porterhouse, cut into 1.5 cm cubes

1 zucchini, halved lengthways, then cut into 1 cm slices

1 green capsicum, cut into 2 cm cubes

1 red capsicum, cut into 2 cm cubes

1 small sweet potato, cut into 2 cm cubes and blanched until just tender

Mix the soy sauce, sesame oil and ginger together in a small bowl. Place the beef in a large container with a lid. Pour over the marinade and cover. Shake the container to ensure the beef is well coated in the marinade. Refrigerate for 2–3 hours, shaking occasionally to evenly coat with the marinade.

If using wooden skewers soak them in water for 10 minutes to prevent scorching.

Remove the beef from the refrigerator. Thread the prepared vegetables and beef onto the skewers.

Preheat a grill plate, chargrill pan or barbecue grill to medium–high and cook the skewers for 5–10 minutes or until just cooked through.

MAKES 12

LASAGNE

- 2 tablespoons garlic-infused olive oil *
- 1 kg lean beef mince
- 300 g lean bacon, diced
- 2 teaspoons cayenne pepper
- 1 teaspoon oregano, chopped
- 1 teaspoon thyme leaves
- ½ teaspoon chilli powder (optional)
- salt and freshly ground black pepper
- 685 mL (2¾ cups) tomato purée
- 1 carrot, peeled and grated
- 1 litre (4 cups) lactose-free milk
- 3 tablespoons gluten-free cornflour
- 300 g (3 cups) grated reduced-fat tasty cheddar
- 1 packet dried rice paper sheets

** Please refer to note on garlic-infused olive oil under heading 'A few specific notes about low-FODMAP cooking', page 89.*

Preheat the oven to 180°C.

Heat the olive oil in a large heavy-based frying pan, add the mince and bacon and sauté until the mince browns. Add the herbs and spices, tomato purée and carrot. Simmer over a medium heat for 10 minutes, stirring occasionally.

In a small mixing bowl, combine 60 mL (¼ cup) of the milk with the cornflour to form a paste. Add the remaining milk, mixing well. Pour into a saucepan and stir until it thickens. Do not boil. Add the cheese and stir until it melts.

Dip the rice paper sheets into a large bowl of water and soak until just flexible. Drain off any excess water.

Using 3 sheets per layer, place a layer of rice paper on the base of a 36 cm x 25 cm lasagne dish. Spread half the meat mixture evenly over the rice paper. Top with one-third of the cheese sauce. Repeat with another layer of rice paper, meat sauce and cheese sauce. Finish with a layer of rice paper and cheese sauce.

Bake in the oven for 20 minutes or until the top is golden brown.

SERVES 8

IF YOU CAN TOLERATE

MANNITOL, *consider adding 150 g sliced* **button mushrooms** *to the recipe.*

LACTOSE, *use* **regular** *rather than* **lactose-free milk.**

FRUCTANS, *consider using one of the following: 1 clove* **garlic,** *crushed and sautéed in olive oil, rather than garlic-infused olive oil; or* **regular** *lasagne sheets rather than rice paper sheets (if you are not also gluten-free).*

MINI QUICHES

PASTRY

- 140 g (1 cup) fine rice flour
- 90 g (½ cup) gluten-free cornflour, plus extra for kneading
- 45 g soy flour *
- 1 teaspoon xanthan gum
- 160 g cold butter
- 80–100 mL iced water

FILLING

- 1 potato, peeled and cut into 5 mm cubes
- 1½ tablespoons garlic-infused olive oil **
- 6 eggs
- 250 mL (1 cup) lactose-free cream
- 250 g chopped cooked spinach
- 100 g (1 cup) grated reduced-fat cheddar cheese
- salt and freshly ground black pepper

** Please refer to note on soy flour under heading 'A few specific notes about low-FODMAP cooking', page 89.*

*** Please refer to note on garlic-infused olive oil under heading 'A few specific notes about low-FODMAP cooking', page 89.*

To make the Pastry, process the sifted flours, xanthan gum and butter in a food processor until the mixture resembles fine breadcrumbs. Continue processing and add the iced water, 1 tablespoon at a time, until the mixture forms a soft dough. (Less water will be required in a warm kitchen.) Turn out the dough onto a board dusted with gluten-free cornflour and knead for 1–2 minutes. Wrap in plastic wrap and rest in the refrigerator for 30 minutes.

Preheat the oven to 170°C. Grease two 12-hole patty pan trays or muffin trays.

Roll out the pastry between two sheets of non-stick baking paper until 2–3 mm thick. Use a round pastry cutter to cut pastry circles large enough to cover the base and sides of the patty pan holes or muffin tray. Ease the pastry circles gently into the pans.

To make the Filling, cook the potato in boiling water until just tender. Drain.

Heat the olive oil in a non-stick frying pan over a medium heat. Add the potato and cook, stirring, for 3–4 minutes or until golden brown.

Whisk the eggs in a mixing bowl, then add the cream, spinach, cheddar, salt and pepper.

Distribute the potatoes evenly among the pastry cases and pour over the egg mixture. Bake for 10–15 minutes or until cooked through and the tops are set when the trays are shaken gently.

MAKES 24

IF YOU CAN TOLERATE

LACTOSE, *use* ***regular*** *rather than lactose-free cream.*

FRUCTANS, *consider using one of the following: ½ clove* ***garlic****, crushed and sautéed in olive oil, rather than garlic-infused olive oil; or store-bought, ready-made* ***wheat-based puff pastries*** *instead of the handmade pastries in recipe (if you are not also gluten-free).*

DESSERTS

CHOCOLATE PUDDINGS

- 35 g (⅓ cup) cocoa powder
- 85 mL (⅓ cup) water
- 150 g unsalted butter
- 150 g dark cooking chocolate
- 275 g (1¼ cups) brown sugar, firmly packed
- 120 g hazelnut meal
- 4 eggs, separated
- halved strawberries, to serve
- ice-cream or cream (lactose-free if desired), to serve
- pure icing sugar

Preheat the oven to 150°C. Grease eight 200 mL ramekins.

In a small saucepan over low heat, combine the cocoa powder, water, butter and chocolate until melted and smooth in consistency. Remove from the heat, stir in the brown sugar, almond meal and egg yolks. Transfer to a large bowl and leave to cool to room temperature.

Beat the egg whites in a small bowl using an electric mixer until soft peaks form. Fold the egg whites into the chocolate mixture in 2 batches.

Pour the mixture into the ramekins. Bake, uncovered, for 20–25 minutes, or when a skewer inserted into the middle comes out clean.

Serve hot with halved strawberries, ice-cream or cream. Dust with pure icing sugar if desired.

SERVES 4

BERRY CRUMBLE

- 500 g (1 bunch) rhubarb, cut into 3 cm pieces
- 110 g (½ cup) caster sugar
- 1 x 410 g can raspberries in syrup, drained
- 200 g blueberries
- 200 g strawberries, hulled and sliced
- 55 g (¼ cup) caster sugar (extra)
- 140 g (1 cup) fine rice flour
- 125 g (⅔ cup) brown sugar, lightly packed
- 3 tablespoons desiccated coconut
- 70 g butter, cubed, at room temperature
- lactose-free cream or ice cream

Preheat the oven to 180°C. Grease a 25 cm round baking dish.

Put the rhubarb in a saucepan with the caster sugar and some water and cook until just tender. Drain off any excess liquid.

Combine the cooked rhubarb, raspberries, blueberries, strawberries and extra caster sugar in a medium-sized bowl. Stir until well combined. Spoon into the baking dish.

In a small bowl, combine the rice flour, brown sugar and coconut. Rub in the butter until the mixture resembles fine breadcrumbs. Sprinkle evenly over the fruit. Bake for 30 minutes or until golden brown. Serve immediately with lactose-free cream or ice cream, if desired.

SERVES 8

IF YOU CAN TOLERATE

LACTOSE, *you may substitute* ***regular cream*** *or* ***ice cream*** *for lactose-free.*

SORBITOL, *you may substitute* ***blackberries*** *for strawberries.*

EXCESS FRUCTOSE, *you may substitute* ***boysenberries*** *for the strawberries.*

EXCESS FRUCTOSE and SORBITOL, *you may substitute* ***apple*** *for the* ***rhubarb****.*

FRUCTANS, *you may substitute 150 g (1 cup)* ***wheat flour*** *for the fine rice flour (if you are not also gluten-free).*

PASSIONFRUIT BRÛLÉE

- 600 mL lactose-free cream
- 6 egg yolks
- 75 g (1/3 cup) caster sugar
- 85 mL passionfruit pulp in syrup (strain, reserving the pips)
- 75 g (1/3 cup) caster sugar (extra)

Preheat the oven to 150°C. Place four 125 mL (½ cup) ramekins in a baking dish.

Pour the cream into a saucepan and stir over a medium heat for 3 minutes. Do not boil. Remove from the heat and cool to room temperature.

Beat the egg yolks and sugar using electric beaters until pale and creamy. Add the cooled cream and passionfruit pulp (plus some of the pips) and beat until well combined.

Divide the passionfruit mixture among the ramekins, filling to three-quarters full. Pour enough boiling water into the baking dish to come two-thirds of the way up the sides of the ramekins. Bake on the lowest shelf of the oven for 40–45 minutes, or until the brûlées are firm around the edges.

Remove the ramekins from the baking dish and set aside to cool to room temperature (this will take about an hour). Cover with plastic wrap and place in the refrigerator for 8 hours or overnight to set.

Sprinkle the remaining sugar over the brûlées and place under a hot grill for about 1 minute until the sugar bubbles and caramelises. (Alternatively, use a kitchen blowtorch to do this.) Set aside for 5 minutes before serving.

SERVES 4

IF YOU CAN TOLERATE

LACTOSE, *use **regular** rather than lactose-free cream.*

STRAWBERRY AND HAZELNUT CAKE

160 g unsalted butter, cubed
275 g (1¼ cups) caster sugar
2 teaspoons vanilla essence
3 eggs
105 g (¾ cup) fine rice flour
20 g (¼ cup) soy flour *
60 g (⅓ cup) gluten-free cornflour
1 teaspoon ground cinnamon
1 teaspoon bicarbonate of soda
2 teaspoons gluten-free baking powder
1 teaspoon xanthan gum
110 g (1 cup) hazelnut meal
250 mL (1 cup) lactose-free cream
110 g (⅓ cup) strawberry jam
icing sugar, for dusting

FILLING

125 mL (½ cup) thickened cream, whipped ** †
2 teaspoons pure icing sugar
1 teaspoon vanilla essence
200 g strawberries, hulled and roughly chopped

** Please refer to note on soy flour under heading 'A few specific notes about low-FODMAP cooking', page 89.*

*** Please refer to note on lactose-free cream under heading 'A few specific notes about low-FODMAP cooking', page 89.*

† If lactose intolerant, you may omit cream from filling or serve yourself a very small slice.

Preheat the oven to 180°C. Grease and line two 20 cm sponge tins.

Use electric beaters to beat the butter, caster sugar and vanilla in a bowl until thick, pale and creamy. Add the eggs, one at a time, beating well after each addition.

Sift the flours, cinnamon, bicarbonate of soda, baking powder and xanthan gum three times into a medium-sized bowl. Alternatively, mix together with a whisk until well combined. Add the hazelnut meal and stir to combine.

Using a large metal spoon, gently fold the flour into the butter mixture, alternating with the cream. Spoon the mixture into the prepared tins.

Bake in the oven for 25–30 minutes or until a skewer inserted into the centre of each cake comes out clean. Allow to cool for 10 minutes in the tins before tipping out to cool completely on wire racks.

To make the Filling, combine the cream, icing sugar, vanilla and strawberries. Mix until well combined.

To assemble, spread the jam over the top of one of the cakes. Top with the filling and then with the second cake. Dust with icing sugar to serve.

SERVES 12–14

IF YOU CAN TOLERATE

SORBITOL, *you may substitute* ***apricots*** *or* ***blackberries*** *for the strawberries.*

EXCESS FRUCTOSE, *you may substitute* ***boysenberries*** *for the strawberries.*

LACTOSE, *you may use* ***regular cream*** *rather than lactose-free, and enjoy a full serving with cream in the filling.*

FRUCTANS, *you may substitute 200 g (1⅓ cups)* ***wheat flour*** *for the rice, soy and corn flours and omit the xanthan gum (if you are not also gluten-free).*

SALTED CARAMEL CUSTARD PUDDINGS

- 185 mL (¾ cup) lactose-free milk
- 310 mL (1¼ cups) lactose-free cream *
- 150 g (¾ cup) brown sugar, lightly packed
- ½ teaspoon salt
- 3 tablespoons gluten-free cornflour
- 60 mL (¼ cup) lactose-free milk (extra)
- lactose-free cream, to serve (optional)
- sliced strawberries, to serve

** Please refer to note on lactose-free cream under heading 'A few specific notes about low-FODMAP cooking', page 89.*

Heat the milk, cream and brown sugar in a saucepan over a medium heat until almost boiling. Stir in the salt. Mix the cornflour in the extra milk to form a smooth paste. Add slowly into the milk and cream mixture, stirring constantly to ensure a smooth consistency. Heat, stirring constantly, for 5 minutes or until it thickens. Do not boil. Pour into four 125 mL (½ cup) ramekins. Allow to cool then cover with plastic wrap and refrigerate for 3–4 hours or until set. Remove from the fridge and serve the ramekin on a plate with a drizzle of lactose-free cream and strawberries.

SERVES 4

IF YOU CAN TOLERATE

LACTOSE, *use* ***regular*** *rather than lactose-free milk and cream.*

TOASTED COCONUT RICE

- 165 g (¾ cup) caster sugar
- 750 mL (3 cups) lactose-free milk (additional as required)
- 400 mL light coconut milk
- 2 teaspoons vanilla essence
- 300 g (1⅓ cups) arborio rice
- 4 tablespoons shredded coconut
- 1 kaffir lime leaf, extremely thinly sliced

Place the sugar, milk, coconut milk and vanilla in a medium-sized saucepan over a medium–high heat and bring to the boil, stirring regularly. Add the rice. Reduce the heat and simmer, stirring regularly, for about 50 minutes or until the liquid is absorbed and the rice is tender. Add extra milk if required.

Meanwhile, preheat the oven to 170°C. Line a baking tray with foil.

Scatter the shredded coconut over the tray and bake for 10–12 minutes or until just starting to turn golden brown.

Serve the rice pudding warm or at room temperature topped with the toasted coconut and a small sprinkling of kaffir lime leaf.

SERVES 6

IF YOU CAN TOLERATE

LACTOSE, *use* ***regular*** *rather than lactose-free milk.*

LEMON SOUFFLÉ

- butter, for greasing
- 120 g caster sugar, plus extra for coating
- 3 tablespoons gluten-free cornflour
- 125 mL (½ cup) lactose-free milk
- 3 eggs, separated
- grated zest of 1 lemon
- juice of 2 lemons

Preheat the oven to 170°C. Grease four 250 mL (1 cup) soufflé dishes with butter, and coat the base and sides evenly with caster sugar.

Combine the cornflour with 1 tablespoon of the milk and 1 egg yolk in a small bowl.

Heat the remaining milk and the lemon zest and juice in a small saucepan over a medium heat until the mixture just comes to the boil (the mixture will appear curdled, but this is fine). Remove from the heat and stir in the cornflour mixture. Return to the stovetop and cook over a low heat until the custard thickens, stirring constantly.

In a separate bowl, mix together 60 g of the sugar and the remaining egg yolks until well combined. Add to the lemon custard and stir through to combine well, ensuring an even consistency.

In a large bowl, beat the egg whites until stiff peaks form. Add the remaining sugar and beat until it dissolves. Gently fold the lemon custard into the egg whites with a large metal spoon, ensuring it is well combined.

Spoon the mixture into the prepared dishes, filling them to the top, then level with a spatula. Bake for 14–17 minutes until the soufflés rise. Serve immediately.

SERVES 4

IF YOU CAN TOLERATE

LACTOSE, *use* ***regular*** *rather than lactose-free milk.*

CHILLI CHOCOLATE CHEESECAKE

- 250 g sweet gluten-free biscuits, crushed
- 3 tablespoons butter, melted
- 125 mL (½ cup) boiling water
- 2 teaspoons gelatine powder
- 250 g lactose-free cream cheese, at room temperature †
- 165 g (¾ cup) caster sugar
- 125 g dark couverture chocolate, melted
- 2 teaspoons ground cinnamon
- ¼ teaspoon chilli powder
- 375 mL (1½ cups) cream*

** Please refer to note on lactose-free cream under heading 'A few specific notes about low-FODMAP cooking', page 89. The amount of regular cream used in this recipe should be tolerated by those with lactose intolerance.*

† If you are lactose intolerant, and can't find lactose-free cream cheese, then use regular cream cheese and enjoy only a small serve.

Mix the crushed biscuits and melted butter together in a small bowl. Press into the base of a 20 cm springform cake tin. Refrigerate for 30 minutes or until firm.

Combine the boiling water and gelatine in a small heatproof bowl. Set the bowl over a larger bowl of boiling water, stirring constantly until all the gelatine dissolves.

Beat the cream cheese, gelatine mixture, sugar, melted chocolate, cinnamon and chilli powder in a small bowl using electric beaters until smooth and creamy, 3–4 minutes.

Beat the cream using electric beaters until thick. Using a large metal spoon, fold the cream into the cream cheese mixture, ensuring it is well combined. Pour the filling over the prepared base, smooth the surface with a spatula, cover and refrigerate for 3 hours or until set.

SERVES 12

IF YOU CAN TOLERATE

LACTOSE, *you may use* **regular** *rather than lactose-free cream cheese, and enjoy a full serving.*

FRUCTANS, *you may substitute* **wheat-based sweet biscuits** *for the gluten-free biscuits (if you are not also gluten-free).*

LIME TART

PASTRY

- 140 g (1 cup) fine rice flour
- 90 g (½ cup) gluten-free cornflour
- 40 g (½ cup) soy flour, plus extra for dusting *
- 1 teaspoon xanthan gum
- 55 g (¼ cup) caster sugar
- 160 g cold butter, chopped
- 100–120 mL (5–6 tablespoons) iced water

FILLING

- 165 g (¾ cup) caster sugar
- 1–2 tablespoons finely grated lime zest
- 165 mL (⅔ cup) fresh lime juice
- 200 g mascarpone
- 4 eggs
- whipped cream, to garnish †
- maple syrup, to garnish
- lime zest, to garnish
- pure icing sugar, to dust

** Please refer to note on soy flour under heading 'A few specific notes about low-FODMAP cooking', page 89.*

† For people with lactose intolerance, restrict the whipped cream garnish to only 1 tablespoon per serve.

Preheat the oven to 180°C. Grease a 23 cm fluted tart tin.

To make the Pastry, combine the flours and xanthan gum in a food processor. Process for 10 seconds to ensure they are well combined. Add the sugar and butter and process until the mixture resembles fine breadcrumbs. While the motor is running, add enough iced water (1 tablespoon at a time) to allow the mixture to form a soft dough. Knead on a benchtop dusted with gluten-free cornflour. Wrap in plastic wrap and refrigerate for 30 minutes before rolling out.

Roll out the pastry between two sheets of non-stick baking paper until it is large enough to line the base and side of the dish, about 2 mm thick. Ease into the dish and trim the edges to neaten. Place a sheet of baking paper over the pastry and put some pastry weights (or rice or dried beans) on top to prevent the pastry shell from rising during cooking. Bake for 10 minutes or until lightly browned. Remove the baking paper and weights and cool.

Lower the oven temperature to 160°C.

To make the Filling, beat the caster sugar, lime zest and juice and mascarpone in a small bowl. Add the eggs, one at a time, beating well after each addition.

Pour into the pastry base and bake for 30–35 minutes or until set. Allow to cool in the tin before serving. Dust with icing sugar and garnish with whipped cream, a drizzle of maple syrup and a sprinkle of lime zest.

SERVES 8–10

IF YOU CAN TOLERATE

FRUCTANS, *you may substitute 300 g (2 cups) plain* ***wheat flour*** *for the rice, corn and soy rice flours and omit the xanthan gum (if you are not also gluten-free).*

BASIL-INFUSED PANNA COTTA

- 165 mL (⅔ cup) lactose-free cream
- 420 mL (1⅔ cups) lactose-free milk
- 110 g (½ cup) caster sugar
- 6–8 torn basil leaves or ¼ cup mint leaves
- 1 tablespoon boiling water
- 2¼ teaspoons gelatine powder
- blueberries, to serve (optional)
- basil or mint leaves (extra), to garnish

Grease four 125 mL (½ cup) dariole moulds.

Heat the cream, milk, sugar and basil leaves in a medium-sized saucepan for 5 minutes – be sure not to boil. Reduce the heat to very low and keep cooking without boiling, stirring regularly, for 20 minutes. Remove from the heat and discard the basil leaves. Set aside.

Combine the boiling water and gelatine in a small heatproof bowl. Set the bowl over a larger bowl of boiling water, stirring constantly until all the gelatine dissolves.

Whisk the gelatine mixture into the cream mixture and pour into a medium-sized bowl.

Fill a large bowl with ice cubes and set the bowl of cream mixture on top. Whisk every few minutes for about 10 minutes; the mixture will thicken as it cools. When the mixture coats the back of a wooden spoon, pour it into the greased moulds.

Refrigerate for 2–3 hours or overnight.

To serve, dip each mould into a bowl of hot water for a few seconds, turn out onto serving plates, serve with blueberries, if desired, and garnish with basil leaves.

SERVES 4

IF YOU CAN TOLERATE

LACTOSE, *use* ***regular*** *rather than lactose-free milk and cream.*

VANILLA PANNA COTTA WITH RASPBERRY COULIS

420 mL (1⅔ cups) lactose-free cream *

125 mL (½ cup) lactose-free milk

110 g (½ cup) caster sugar

2 vanilla bean pods – split and scrape seeds to use, or 2 teaspoons vanilla bean paste

1 tablespoon boiling water

2¼ teaspoons gelatine powder

RASPBERRY COULIS

300 g fresh raspberries, rinsed

125 mL (½ cup) water

60 g (½ cup) pure icing sugar, sifted

Or, use 1 x 410 g can raspberries, retaining 80 mL (⅓ cup) syrup

** Please refer to note on lactose-free cream under heading 'A few specific notes about low-FODMAP cooking', page 89.*

Grease four 125 mL (½ cup) dariole moulds.

Heat the cream, milk, sugar and vanilla bean seeds or paste in a medium-sized saucepan over a low heat. Cook, stirring regularly, for 20 minutes. Do not boil. Remove from the heat.

Combine the boiling water and gelatine in a small heatproof bowl. Set the bowl over a larger bowl of boiling water, stirring constantly until all the gelatine dissolves.

Whisk the gelatine mixture into the cream mixture, and pour into a medium bowl.

Fill a large bowl with ice cubes and set the bowl of cream mixture on top. Whisk every few minutes for about 10 minutes; the mixture will thicken as it cools. When the mixture coats the back of a wooden spoon, pour it into the greased moulds.

Refrigerate for 2–3 hours.

To make the Raspberry Coulis, place the raspberries, water and icing sugar in a small saucepan over medium heat and simmer for 5 minutes until raspberries soften and break up (or heat canned raspberries and some syrup, if using). Turn heat to low and stir regularly until coulis has reduced and thickened slightly. Press through a fine wire sieve and pour into an airtight container and chill for at least 1 hour. Unused coulis can be frozen.

To serve, dip each mould into a bowl of hot water for a few seconds, then turn out onto serving plates. Drizzle over the raspberry coulis.

SERVES 4

IF YOU CAN TOLERATE

SORBITOL, *you may substitute* ***blackberries*** *for raspberries.*

EXCESS FRUCTOSE, *you may substitute* ***boysenberries*** *for raspberries.*

LACTOSE, *use* ***regular*** *rather than lactose-free milk and cream.*

PANCAKES WITH STRAWBERRIES, MASCARPONE AND MAPLE SYRUP

- 85 g (⅔ cup) fine rice flour
- 20 g (¼ cup) soy flour *
- 50 g gluten-free cornflour
- ¾ teaspoon bicarbonate of soda
- 2½ tablespoons caster sugar
- 1 egg, lightly beaten
- 65 mL (⅔ cup) lactose-free milk
- 2 tablespoons butter, melted
- non-stick cooking oil spray
- 4 tablespoons mascarpone, to serve
- maple syrup, to serve

STRAWBERRY SAUCE

- 250 g strawberries, hulled
- juice of 1 lemon
- 110 g (½ cup) caster sugar

** Please refer to note on soy flour under heading 'A few specific notes about low-FODMAP cooking', page 89.*

Sift the flours and bicarbonate of soda three times into a bowl (or mix well with a whisk to ensure they are well combined), then add the sugar.

Whisk together the beaten egg and milk and pour into the dry ingredients. Mix with a spoon until well combined. Stir in the melted butter, cover and set aside for 10 minutes.

To make the Strawberry Sauce, place the strawberries, lemon juice and caster sugar in a food processor and blend until the sugar dissolves and the purée is smooth and glossy. Place in a saucepan and heat for 6–8 minutes or until thickened slightly.

Heat a frying pan over a medium–low heat for 2 minutes. Spray with cooking oil spray, then add 3–4 tablespoons batter for each pancake. Cook for 2–3 minutes until bubbles start to appear, then flip over and cook for 2 minutes. Remove from the pan and keep warm while you make the remaining pancakes. Serve with strawberry sauce, a dollop of mascarpone and a drizzle of maple syrup.

MAKES 6–8

IF YOU CAN TOLERATE

SORBITOL, *you may substitute* ***blackberries*** *for the strawberries.*

EXCESS FRUCTOSE, *you may substitute* ***boysenberries*** *for the strawberries.*

LACTOSE, *use* ***regular*** *rather than lactose-free milk.*

FRUCTANS, *you may substitute 190 g (1¼ cups)* ***wheat flour*** *for the rice, soy and corn flours (if you are not also gluten-free).*

CHOCOLATE HAZELNUT MOUSSE

- 60 mL (¼ cup) boiling water
- 1½ teaspoons gelatine powder
- 200 g good-quality dark cooking chocolate
- 150 mL thickened cream, plus extra to serve * †
- 3 tablespoons hazelnut liqueur, e.g. Frangelico
- 3 eggs, separated
- 2 tablespoons caster sugar
- cocoa powder, to dust

** Please refer to note on lactose-free cream under heading 'A few specific notes about low-FODMAP cooking', page 89.*

† If you are lactose intolerant, enjoy only a small serve.

Combine the boiling water and gelatine in a small heatproof bowl. Set the bowl over a larger bowl of boiling water, stirring constantly until all the gelatine dissolves.

Combine the chocolate and cream in a heatproof bowl. Place the bowl over a saucepan of simmering water, ensuring the base doesn't touch the water, and stir until melted. Cool to room temperature, then stir in the gelatine mixture and hazelnut liqueur, mixing well. Add the egg yolks, one at a time, stirring well to combine.

Place the egg whites in a small clean bowl and beat using an electric beater until soft peaks form. Add the sugar and beat until it dissolves.

Using a large metal spoon, gently fold the egg whites into the chocolate mixture in 2 batches. Pour the mixture into four 165 mL (⅔ cup) serving dishes or glasses and refrigerate for 3–4 hours or overnight. Serve with a spoonful of cream if desired, and a dusting of cocoa.

SERVES 4

IF YOU CAN TOLERATE

LACTOSE, *enjoy a full serve.*

COFFEE CRÈME CARAMEL WITH CHOCOLATE SAUCE

COFFEE CRÈME CARAMEL

- 500 mL (2 cups) lactose-free milk
- 2 teaspoons coffee powder
- 1 teaspoon vanilla essence
- 4 eggs
- 1 tablespoon caster sugar

CHOCOLATE SAUCE

- 60 g (1/3 cup) brown sugar, lightly packed
- 2 tablespoons cocoa powder, sifted
- 1¼ tablespoons gluten-free cornflour
- 375 mL (1½ cups) lactose-free milk
- 2 tablespoons coffee liqueur, e.g. Kahlua or Tia Maria (optional)
- 4 tablespoons lactose-free cream (optional)

Preheat the oven to 160°C. Grease four 125 mL (½ cup) ramekins with butter.

Heat the milk, coffee and vanilla in a medium-sized saucepan over a medium heat for 5 minutes; do not boil. Remove from the heat and set aside.

Beat the eggs and sugar together, and stir into the milk mixture. Pour the mixture through a sieve into the greased ramekins.

Place a folded tea-towel in the base of a baking dish. Place the ramekins on top and add hot water to come two-thirds of the way up the sides of the ramekins to make a water bath. Cook for 20–25 minutes or until set (a knife inserted in the centre of the crème caramel should come out clean or with only some soft-set custard on the knife).

Remove the ramekins from the water bath and allow to cool to room temperature, then refrigerate overnight or for about 5 hours.

To make the Chocolate Sauce, combine the brown sugar, cocoa powder and cornflour in a small saucepan. Stir in a little of the milk to form a paste, then add the remaining milk and mix well to ensure there are no lumps. Stir over a medium–high heat until the sauce thickens slightly, then remove from the heat and stir in the coffee liqueur, if using. Transfer to a jug, cover and refrigerate until ready to serve.

When set, take the caramels from the refrigerator. Serve in the ramekins, or run a knife around the inside of the ramekins to loosen and invert into four shallow bowls. Add a spoonful of cream, then pour over the sauce.

SERVES 4

IF YOU CAN TOLERATE

LACTOSE, *use regular rather than lactose-free milk and cream.*

LEMON COCONUT CHEESECAKE

- 200 g plain gluten-free sweet biscuits
- 60 g butter, melted
- 125 mL (½ cup) boiling water
- 2 tablespoons gelatine powder
- 250 g mascarpone
- 300 mL lactose-free cream
- 110 g (½ cup) caster sugar
- 125 mL (½ cup) lemon juice
- 2 tablespoons finely grated lemon zest
- 2 tablespoons desiccated coconut
- 2 egg whites, at room temperature
- caramelised lemon slices, to garnish (optional)
- white chocolate curls, to garnish (optional)
- 2 egg whites, at room temperature

Crush the biscuits until they are fine crumbs. Add the butter and stir until well combined. Press evenly into the base of a 23 cm springform cake tin.

Combine the boiling water and gelatine in a small heatproof bowl. Set the bowl over a larger bowl of boiling water, stirring constantly until all the gelatine dissolves.

In a large mixing bowl, beat the mascarpone, cream, 55 g (¼ cup) of the sugar, the lemon juice and zest, coconut and gelatine mixture. Mix until evenly combined. Set aside.

In a separate mixing bowl, beat the egg whites and remaining sugar until soft peaks form. Fold the beaten egg whites into the lemon coconut mixture until well combined.

Pour the filling over the prepared base, and refrigerate until set, 2–3 hours. Garnish with lemon slices and white chocolate curls, if desired.

SERVES 12–14

IF YOU CAN TOLERATE

LACTOSE, *use* ***regular*** *rather than lactose-free cream.*

FRUCTANS, *you may substitute* ***wheat-based sweet biscuits*** *for the gluten-free biscuits (if you are not also gluten-free).*

GINGERBREAD ICE-CREAM COOKIES

- 1 egg
- 80 g (1/3 cup) brown sugar, firmly packed
- 200 g (½ cup) golden syrup
- 80 g butter, melted
- 140 g (1 cup) fine rice flour, plus extra for dusting
- 90 g (½ cup) potato flour
- 80 g (1 cup) soy flour *
- 1 teaspoon xanthan gum
- 1 teaspoon baking powder
- 1–1½ tablespoons ground ginger, or to taste
- 500 mL lactose-free vanilla ice cream
- 2 teaspoons ground ginger, extra

** Please refer to note on soy flour under heading 'A few specific notes about low-FODMAP cooking', page 89.*

Preheat the oven to 150°C. Line three baking trays with baking paper.

Beat the egg and brown sugar together with a wooden spoon. Add the golden syrup and melted butter.

Sift the flours, xanthan gum, baking powder and ginger together three times in a bowl (alternatively use a whisk and combine well in a bowl). Add the flour mixture to the egg mixture and mix well to combine. Refrigerate for 15 minutes.

Remove from the refrigerator: the mixture should be firm. On a board dusted with fine rice flour, roll out the dough to a 2–3 mm thickness. Use cookie cutters to cut to shape. The mixture should make around 30 cookies. Place on the prepared trays (allow room for spreading) and bake for 6–8 minutes, until just turning golden, i.e. just cooked (do not overcook). Remove from the oven and allow to sit on the tray for 10–15 minutes before transferring to wire racks to cool. Set 8 cookies aside and store the remaining cookies in an airtight container for treats at another time.

Remove the ice cream from the freezer and allow to soften a little. Sprinkle the extra ground ginger over the ice cream and quickly stir through, ensuring it is well combined. Place a spoonful of ice cream onto a cookie base and pop a second cookie on top.

SERVES 4 (2 COOKIES PER SERVE)

IF YOU CAN TOLERATE

LACTOSE, *use* ***regular*** *rather than lactose-free ice cream.*

FRUCTANS, *you may substitute 375 g (2½ cups) plain* ***wheat flour or spelt flour*** *for the rice, potato and soy flours and omit the xanthan gum (if you are not also gluten-free).*

BAKED

PECAN AND CINNAMON MUFFINS

- 140 g (1 cup) fine rice flour
- 90 g (½ cup) gluten-free cornflour
- 70 g (½ cup) tapioca flour
- 2 teaspoons ground cinnamon
- 1 teaspoon bicarbonate of soda
- 2 teaspoons gluten-free baking powder
- 1 teaspoon xanthan gum
- 220 g (1 cup) brown sugar, firmly packed
- 90 g (¾ cup) chopped pecans
- 2 small carrots, peeled and grated
- 125 mL (½ cup) vegetable oil
- 3 eggs, lightly beaten
- 125 mL (½ cup) lactose-free milk

Preheat the oven to 170°C. Grease and line a 12-hole muffin tin with baking paper, or use paper cases.

Sift together the flours, cinnamon, bicarbonate of soda, baking powder and xanthan gum three times, or mix well with a whisk to ensure they are well combined. Stir in the sugar and pecans. Add the carrots, vegetable oil, eggs and milk and mix until just combined with a wooden spoon.

Spoon the batter into the paper cases and smooth the tops. Bake for 12–16 minutes until golden brown (a skewer inserted into the centre of a muffin should come out clean). Remove from the oven and leave to cool in the tin for 10 minutes before transferring to a wire rack to cool completely.

MAKES 10–12

IF YOU CAN TOLERATE

LACTOSE, *use* ***regular*** *rather than lactose-free milk.*

FRUCTANS, *you may substitute 300 g (2 cups) plain* ***wheat flour*** *or spelt flour for the rice, corn and tapioca flours and omit the xanthan gum (if you are not also gluten-free).*

RED VELVET CUPCAKES

- 140 g (1 cup) fine rice flour
- 70 g (½ cup) tapioca flour
- 90 g (½ cup) gluten-free cornflour
- 2½ teaspoons gluten-free baking powder
- 2 teaspoons bicarbonate of soda
- 1 teaspoon xanthan gum
- 2 tablespoons cocoa powder
- 2 tablespoons butter, melted
- 200 g (¾ cup) lactose- and gluten-free vanilla yoghurt
- 1 teaspoon vanilla essence
- 1½ teaspoons red food colouring
- 2 eggs
- 180 g caster sugar

CREAM CHEESE ICING

- 225 g reduced-fat, lactose-free cream cheese
- 1½ tablespoons fresh lemon juice
- 80 g icing sugar

Preheat the oven to 180°C. Place paper cases into a 12-hole muffin tray.

Sift the flours, baking powder, bicarbonate of soda, xanthan gum and cocoa powder three times into a large mixing bowl.

In a medium-sized mixing bowl, combine the melted butter, yoghurt, vanilla, red food colouring, eggs and sugar. Mix well, and add this mixture to the flour mixture. Mix well with a metal spoon until just combined.

Fill each paper case with batter until two-thirds full. Cook for 20–22 minutes until a skewer comes out clean when inserted into the centre of one of the cupcakes. Cool on a wire rack.

To make the **Cream Cheese Icing**, use an electric mixer to beat all the ingredients together in a small bowl until smooth.

Top the cooled cupcakes with the icing and serve.

MAKES 12

IF YOU CAN TOLERATE

LACTOSE, *use* ***regular*** *rather than lactose-free yoghurt and cream cheese.*

FRUCTANS, *you may substitute 2 cups plain* ***wheat flour*** *or spelt flour for the fine corn, rice and tapioca flours and omit xanthan gum (if you are not also gluten-free).*

MACARONS

- 2 egg whites
- 60 g (½ cup) pure icing sugar
- 1 teaspoon vanilla bean paste
- 100 g (1 cup) finely ground almond meal

FILLING

- 200 g white chocolate buttons
- 2 different colouring powders (for colouring white chocolate)
- 2 tablespoons lactose-free cream

Preheat the oven to 160°C. Line two baking trays with baking paper.

Place the egg whites into a large bowl and beat using electric beaters for 4–5 minutes or until soft peaks just start to form. Add the sugar and vanilla and continue beating until the sugar dissolves and soft peaks have formed. Do not overbeat.

Sift the almond meal over the egg whites and gently fold through.

Use a teaspoon to drop the macaron mixture onto the baking trays, allowing room for the batter to spread. Allow to stand for 5 minutes. Shape the batter into even round-edged circles if needed.

Bake for 10–14 minutes (varies according to size of macaron), or until crisp on the outside and just turning a very light golden brown.

Remove from the oven and allow to cool on the baking trays. Transfer to wire racks using an egg slice until ready to assemble.

To make the Filling, melt the chocolate in a small glass bowl set over a saucepan of simmering water, ensuring the base of the bowl does not touch the water. When melted, divide in half. Add one colouring powder and 1 tablespoon cream to one half of the chocolate. Mix to combine well and ensure it is coloured evenly. Add the other colouring powder and the remaining cream to the remaining chocolate and mix well. Allow the coloured chocolate to cool and become slightly thickened.

To assemble, turn a macaron upside down and spread some of the coloured chocolate on to the base. Place another same-sized macaron on top and sandwich together to ensure some of the filling comes to the edge. Set aside to allow the chocolate to set. Repeat for remaining macarons.

MAKES 16

IF YOU CAN TOLERATE

LACTOSE, *use* ***regular*** *rather than lactose-free cream.*

BANANA CORNBREAD

- cooking oil spray
- 105 g (¾ cup) fine rice flour
- 35 g (¼ cup) tapioca flour
- 1 teaspoon xanthan gum
- 3½ teaspoons gluten-free baking powder
- 190 g (1 cup) polenta
- 2 tablespoons caster sugar, or more to taste
- 250 mL (1 cup) coconut milk
- 1 banana, mashed
- 3 tablespoons crème fraîche
- 1 tablespoon canola oil
- 1 egg, lightly beaten

Preheat the oven to 195°C. Spray a shallow 20 cm square baking tin with cooking oil spray.

Mix the flours, xanthan gum, baking powder, polenta and sugar in a large mixing bowl with a whisk to ensure they are well combined.

In a small bowl, combine the coconut milk, banana, crème fraîche, canola oil and egg until well mixed. Add the coconut milk mixture to the dry ingredients and mix well to combine.

Pour the mixture into the prepared tin and bake for 25–30 minutes until a skewer comes out clean when inserted in the centre. Leave to cool in the tin for 5 minutes, then transfer to a wire rack to cool completely.

SERVES 12

IF YOU CAN TOLERATE

FRUCTANS, *you may substitute 150 g (1 cup) plain* ***wheat flour*** *or spelt flour for the fine rice and tapioca flours and omit the xanthan gum (if you are not also gluten-free).*

RHUBARB AND COCONUT CAKE

500 g (1 bunch) rhubarb, cut into 3 cm pieces
110 g (½ cup) caster sugar
140 g (1 cup) fine rice flour
45 g (¼ cup) gluten-free cornflour
20 g (¼ cup) soy flour *
1½ teaspoons gluten-free baking powder
1 teaspoon xanthan gum
90 g (1 cup) desiccated coconut
220 g (1 cup) caster sugar, extra
250 mL (1 cup) lactose-free milk
2 eggs, lightly beaten
2 tablespoons vegetable oil
pure icing sugar, for dusting

** Please refer to note on soy flour under heading 'A few specific notes about low-FODMAP cooking', page 89.*

Preheat the oven to 170°C. Grease and line the base of a 22 cm springform tin.

Simmer the rhubarb with the sugar in a large saucepan of boiling water until tender. Drain. Reserve a few pieces for decoration.

Sift the flours, baking powder and xanthan gum into a large bowl. Add the coconut and extra caster sugar, mixing until well combined.

In a small bowl, whisk together the milk, eggs and vegetable oil. Pour into the dry ingredients and mix well to combine, ensuring there are no lumps. Stir through the cooked rhubarb.

Pour into the prepared tin and bake for 55–60 minutes, until a skewer inserted in the centre comes out clean. Cool in the tin for 5 minutes, then turn out onto a wire rack and cool completely. Decorate with reserved rhubarb and dust with icing sugar before serving.

SERVES 12

IF YOU CAN TOLERATE

SORBITOL, *you may substitute* ***blackberries*** *for the rhubarb.*

EXCESS FRUCTOSE, *you may substitute* ***boysenberries*** *for the rhubarb.*

LACTOSE, *use* ***regular*** *rather than lactose-free milk.*

FRUCTANS, *you may substitute 225 g (1½ cups) plain* ***wheat flour*** *or spelt flour for the rice, corn and soy flours and omit the xanthan gum (if you are not also gluten-free).*

CARAMEL POPCORN BARS

- 2½ tablespoons butter
- 2½ tablespoons Copha
- 110 g (½ cup) brown sugar, firmly packed
- 3 tablespoons glucose syrup
- 50 g (4 cups) cooked popcorn

Line a 30 cm × 20 cm lamington tray (shallow baking dish) with baking paper.

Melt the butter and Copha in a large saucepan over a medium heat. Add the brown sugar and glucose syrup and stir until the sugar dissolves. Reduce the heat to medium–low and simmer for 5 minutes or until the sauce has caramelised. Set aside to cool slightly.

Place the popcorn in a large mixing bowl. Pour the sauce over the top and stir well to coat then cool slightly. While still warm, press into the prepared dish, ensuring it is firmly packed. Place in the refrigerator and cool until firm. Remove from the refrigerator and using a sharp knife, cut into 10 cm × 3 cm logs.

MAKES ABOUT 20

IF YOU CAN TOLERATE

FRUCTANS, *consider adding 2 tablespoons* **dried cranberries** *to the mix.*

MANDARIN SYRUP CAKE

- 3 large mandarins
- 125 g (1¼ cups) almond meal
- 1 teaspoon gluten-free baking powder
- 90 g (½ cup) fine rice flour
- 5 eggs
- 275 g (1¼ cups) caster sugar

SYRUP

- grated zest and juice of 1 orange
- 110 g (½ cup) caster sugar
- 165 mL (⅔ cup) water
- 4–5 slices orange, for decoration

Preheat the oven to 170°C. Grease and line 22 cm springform cake tin.

Place the mandarins in a medium-sized saucepan of boiling water. Boil, covered, for 20 minutes. Remove from the heat and drain.

Process the whole mandarins (pips, pith and all!) in a food processor until a smooth paste, 3–4 minutes. Set aside to cool.

Sift the almond meal, baking powder and fine rice flour into a bowl three times.

In a medium-sized bowl, beat the eggs until thick and creamy, about 5 minutes. Slowly add the sugar and beat until well combined.

Stir the mandarin paste into the dry ingredients, mixing well. Fold into the egg mixture with a large metal spoon, ensuring it is well combined.

Pour the mixture into the prepared tin. Cover with foil and bake for 40 minutes.

To make the Syrup, while the cake is baking, place all the ingredients except the orange slices in a saucepan and stir over a medium heat until the sugar dissolves. Bring the mixture to the boil, then reduce the heat to low. Add the orange slices and simmer gently for 10–15 minutes until the syrup thickens and the orange slices are tender.

Remove the foil from the cake and continue to cook for 20 minutes or until golden brown and firm to the touch. A skewer should come out clean when inserted into the centre of the cake. Allow to cool for 15 minutes before removing from the tin. Cool completely on a wire rack. Before serving, decorate with orange slices and drizzle with the syrup.

SERVES 10–12

IF YOU CAN TOLERATE

FRUCTANS, *you may substitute ½ cup* ***plain wheat flour*** *for the fine rice flour (if you are not also gluten-free).*

DOUBLE CHOC CHIP BISCUITS

- 200 g unsalted butter, softened
- 165 g (¾ cup) brown sugar, firmly packed
- 2 eggs
- 175 g (1¼ cup) fine rice flour
- 60 g (⅓ cup) gluten-free cornflour
- 40 g (½ cup) soy flour *
- ½ teaspoon xanthan gum
- 3 tablespoons cocoa powder
- 150 g choc chips

** Please refer to note on soy flour under heading 'A few specific notes about low-FODMAP cooking', page 89.*

Preheat the oven to 180°C and line two baking trays with baking paper.

Beat the butter and brown sugar using electric beaters until creamy. Add the eggs, one at a time, beating well after each addition.

Sift the flours, xanthan gum and cocoa powder three times into a bowl (or mix well with a whisk). Add to the butter mixture and stir until well combined. Mix in the choc chips, then gently bring the dough together with your hands. Roll into golfball-sized balls and place on the trays, about 5 cm apart (to allow for spreading). Flatten slightly with the back of a fork. Dip fork in cocoa powder to prevent sticking.

Bake for 12–15 minutes until browned. Remove from the oven and leave to cool on the trays for 10 minutes before transferring to a wire rack to cool completely.

MAKES 18

IF YOU CAN TOLERATE

FRUCTANS, *you may substitute 300 g (2 cups) plain* ***wheat flour*** *or spelt flour for the rice, corn and soy flours and omit the xanthan gum (if you are not also gluten-free).*

IF YOU CAN TOLERATE

LACTOSE, *use **regular** rather than lactose-free milk and cream.*

FRUCTANS, *you may substitute the rice flour and xanthan gum with 150 g (1 cup) plain **wheat flour** (if you are not also gluten-free).*

CHOCOLATE ÉCLAIRS

CHOUX PASTRY

- 185 mL (¾ cup) water
- 75 g butter
- 140 g (1 cup) fine rice flour
- 1 teaspoon xanthan gum
- 1 tablespoon caster sugar
- 3 eggs

FRENCH CUSTARD

- 250 mL (1 cup) lactose-free milk
- 250 mL (1 cup) lactose-free cream
- 6 egg yolks
- 110 g (½ cup) caster sugar
- 4 tablespoons gluten-free cornflour
- 2 teaspoons vanilla extract or 1–2 teaspoons vanilla bean paste

CHOCOLATE ICING

- 30 g unsalted butter
- 100 g (½ cup) brown sugar, firmly packed
- 60 mL (¼ cup) lactose-free cream
- 2 tablespoons cocoa powder
- ½ cup dark chocolate buttons

Preheat the oven to 200°C. Grease two baking trays.

To make the Choux Pastry, combine the water and butter in a saucepan and bring to the boil. Mix the flour and xanthan gum in a bowl until well combined. Add to the saucepan and beat with a wooden spoon; the mixture will come away from the side of the saucepan and form a smooth ball.

Transfer the dough to a medium-sized bowl, and using electric beaters, beat in the sugar and eggs, one at a time.

Spoon the pastry to a piping bag with an open round nozzle about 1 cm wide. Pipe a log of pastry 10 cm long, and then pipe another log directly on top of it, so it is of double thickness. Repeat with the remaining pastry mix.

Bake for 7 minutes or until the pastries puff up. Reduce the oven temperature to 180°C and bake for a further 10 minutes or until lightly browned and crisp.

Remove one tray from the oven. Quickly and carefully pierce a hole through each éclair from top to tail with a skewer. Return tray to oven and repeat with the second tray. Bake at 140°C for a further 5 minutes or until the éclairs dry out. Cool to room temperature then carefully cut the éclairs in half and open out to cool completely.

To make the French Custard, bring the milk and cream to nearly boiling in a saucepan over a medium heat. Remove from heat. In a large bowl, beat the egg yolks and sugar together using electric beaters until thick and creamy. Beat in the cornflour. Pour the hot milk/cream and vanilla into the bowl and whisk until smooth. Return the mixture to the saucepan and whisk over a medium heat until custard thickens. Pour into a bowl, cover and refrigerate until cold.

To make the Chocolate Icing, melt the butter in a small saucepan over a low heat. Add the brown sugar, cream, cocoa powder and chocolate. Stir over a low heat until the chocolate melts and is smooth. Cool to room temperature until thick and spreadable.

When the éclairs are cool, top one half with French custard and the other with chocolate icing. Place the choc-topped halves on top of the bases with the custard filling.

MAKES 12

CHOCOLATE CAKE

- 140 g (1 cup) fine rice flour
- 90 g (½ cup) gluten-free cornflour
- 90 g (½ cup) potato flour
- 70 g cocoa powder
- 2 teaspoons gluten-free baking powder
- 1 teaspoon bicarbonate of soda
- 1 teaspoon xanthan gum
- 2 eggs
- 330 g (1½ cups) caster sugar
- 50 g butter, melted
- 200 g (¾ cup) lactose- and gluten-free vanilla yoghurt
- 150 mL (⅔ cup) lactose-free milk

CHOCOLATE BUTTER CREAM

- 125 g butter, softened
- 185 g (1½ cup) pure icing sugar
- 4 tablespoons cocoa powder

Preheat the oven to 170°C. Grease a 23 cm springform cake tin.

Measure the flours, cocoa powder, baking powder, bicarbonate of soda and xanthan gum into a large bowl. Mix well with a whisk to ensure they are well combined.

In a medium-sized bowl, beat the eggs and sugar for 2 minutes. Add the melted butter, yoghurt and milk and beat on low speed until just mixed. Add to the flour mixture and beat using electric beaters for 1–2 minutes.

Pour the mixture into the prepared tin and bake for 50–60 minutes until firm to the touch and a skewer comes out clean when inserted into the centre of the cake. Leave to cool in the tin for 5 minutes, then transfer to a wire rack to cool completely.

To make the Chocolate Butter Cream, using an electric mixer beat all ingredients in a small bowl until smooth. To serve, top chocolate cake with the cream.

SERVES 12

IF YOU CAN TOLERATE

LACTOSE, *use* ***regular*** *rather than lactose-free milk and yoghurt.*

FRUCTANS, *you may substitute 300 g (2 cups) plain* ***wheat flour*** *for the rice, corn and potato flours and omit the xanthan gum (if you are not also gluten-free).*

PART 3: USEFUL INFORMATION

FREQUENTLY ASKED QUESTIONS ABOUT THE LOW-FODMAP DIET

Why are low-FODMAP sourdough breads listed in your meal plans – these are often made from wheat, so aren't they high in FODMAPs?

Typically, wheat, rye, barley and spelt flours are all high in FODMAPs. However, if a bread is made using a sourdough process, then the baker can treat the dough to make a final bread that can actually be low in FODMAPs. Many gluten-free breads are also low in FODMAPs. Regular bread making won't usually break down FODMAPs, so it is recommended that breads should be sourdough and labelled as being low-FODMAP or FODMAP Friendly just to be sure they are suitable. Low-FODMAP breads using the FODMAP Friendly logo (described on page 61) are available.

I've completed Step One of the Low-FODMAP Diet and I feel great. Why should I do Step Two?

The goal of the second step is to work through a reintroduction process so that you can enjoy a liberalised diet and increase the variety of foods while still maintaining your symptom control. It's an important step so that your diet isn't unnecessarily restricted. There's no point cutting out more than you need to feel well. Also, we know that FODMAPs are beneficial for the health of the bowel (they act as prebiotics which can assist in the production of products such as short-chain fatty acids which enhance the health of the lining of the bowel wall).

Should I be using probiotics?

Probiotics are live bacteria that can help improve the numbers and balance of good bacteria in the large bowel. Bacteria naturally live in the bowel and are necessary to assist in bowel function and health. An enormous range of strains (types) of bacteria act as probiotics, and they work on the bowel in a variety of ways. A probiotic with bifidobacteria may be helpful if you have completed the Step Two reintroduction process and could not tolerate any high-FODMAP foods well. Speak with your doctor and or specialist dietitian about probiotics, to make sure you're taking the best probiotic for your needs.

What's a normal amount of wind to have? How do I know if mine is a problem?

Here are some fast facts about wind/gas/farts/flatus:

- Babies start passing wind a few days after birth.
- All of us pass wind, though some may try to deny it!
- The amount of gas produced each day can range from 200 ml to 3 litres.
- The amount of gas released each time wind is passed can be 30–120 ml primarily made up of carbon dioxide (CO_2), oxygen (O_2), nitrogen

(N2), hydrogen (H2), and sometimes methane (CH4). The content of the gas differs according to the time of day. An early morning fart is mainly nitrogen, while farts during the day have a higher component of hydrogen and carbon dioxide with the nitrogen. The colon muscles that expel the gas slow down at night.

- The amount of gas being released can influence how loud the flatus is; generally, the more gas there is the louder it is. Your posture can influence the volume -- it is often louder when standing compared to sitting.
- On average, men pass wind twelve times a day and women seven times a day, but the rates may be as high as nearly 40 times a day. It's an unrealistic goal to never want to pass wind again. If, however, you're at the higher end, it may be for a few reasons, including a very high-fibre diet, coeliac disease or malabsorption of some food molecules (such as FODMAPs). Speak to your doctor about your wind if you feel it's excessive – it may indicate an underlying condition.

Must I choose gluten-free foods?

No. Gluten is the *protein* component of wheat, rye and barley (and, in some countries, is considered to be present in oats). This is a very different molecule from FODMAPs, which are *carbohydrates*. As the FODMAP fructans are found in wheat, rye and barley, many gluten-free foods can be suitable, as they're not made from wheat, rye or barley. However, be aware! Not all gluten-free foods are suitable for a Low-FODMAP Diet – a gluten-free apple pie, for example, is not low-FODMAP. Also, people on a Low-FODMAP Diet can eat oats and small amounts of wheat, rye and barley, while people on a gluten-free diet can't have these at all.

I know soy is a legume high in FODMAPs, but what about soy milk? Is there any I can have?

Yes, some soy milks are low in FODMAPs, but it depends on the process involved in making them. The whole soybean contains FODMAPs, so when the whole bean is processed into soy milk, that soy milk will also be high in FODMAPs. Some soy milk manufacturers use a soybean extract that's the protein part of the soybean and therefore leaves behind the part of the legume that contains the FODMAPs. Soy milks made from soy milk protein or soy milk extract are therefore low in FODMAPs and suitable for the diet. Read the ingredients list to determine the soy base the soy milk is made from. The Low-FODMAP Diet Shopping Guide may also assist you, available from www.shepherdworks.com.au

Do I have to be careful of medicines that may contain FODMAPs?

The 'sugar pill' in the contraceptive pill is made from lactose. People with lactose intolerance can handle up to 4 grams of lactose at a time, so given the contraceptive pill doesn't weigh 4 grams, it's fine to continue to take.

FODMAPs in foods are present in much greater amounts than any could be in a medication, so even if a medication contains FODMAPs, they're likely to be well tolerated. Some medications are only taken for a short period of time, and aren't likely to be a bother. If you're taking a medication for an extended period of time that does contain FODMAPs and you feel it is contributing to your symptoms, don't stop taking it, but speak to your doctor about a possible low-FODMAP alternative. If there isn't an alternative, consider further restricting some dietary sources of FODMAPs to assist in minimising your total FODMAP load.

Some cough mixtures that are 'sugar-free' may be sweetened with sorbitol and/or mannitol, sometimes in very high amounts. If these cause you symptoms, you might like to speak to your pharmacist about a brand that doesn't contain polyols.

Can I eat sugar on the Low-FODMAP Diet?

Yes. Sugar is a disaccharide (double sugar) made up of one part fructose, one part glucose. It is in balance, so it is low-FODMAP. Eating sugar in moderation should not trigger symptoms of IBS. Moderate amounts include the amount of sugar you might have in a cake or biscuit in this cookbook (or other low-FODMAP commercially available baked goods), the amount in a serve of chocolate, or the sugar added to tea or coffee. However, just like an orange is a balanced fruit but caution is raised about having too much orange juice due to a high fructose load, a similar caution is needed for sugar. If you are someone who could eat a bag of lollies and cans of soft drink, i.e. lots of sugar at once, you are likely to have symptoms triggered because of too much fructose. Only eat a small handful of confectionery at a time and cap soft drink to no more than 2 small glasses at a time (as described on page 92).

What's the best piece of advice you can you give people about managing a food intolerance and continuing life as normal?

You may feel that your life is anything but normal when you embark on the Low-FODMAP Diet. You may think things that you haven't had to think before. For example, 'Where am I going to be today? Will I need to take food with me? Should I eat before I go? Will there be something that I can have?' Whether you want to or not, you have to think about the food you will be eating. Some people cope with this easily, but for others it really is a big deal.

It can help to:

- Understand your condition – which foods trigger your intolerance or symptoms.
- Seek the advice of an Accredited Practising Dietitian who works in the area of food intolerances to teach you which foods you can still enjoy to ensure your diet is nutritionally adequate.
- Plan your day – make sure you're not going to be caught out without friendly food.
- Educate those around you – the more people who understand your dietary needs, the easier it will be for you. This is important for catering at work conferences, sports events, business meetings, and so on.

Will going on the Low-FODMAP Diet affect my weight?

There has been no hard evidence to show that the Low-FODMAP Diet has a direct effect on weight, leading to weight loss. However anecdotal observations have found that following Step One and Two of the Low-FODMAP Diet generally reduces the number of processed foods eaten, and encourages a shift to healthier food choices. Healthier food choices may also come more easily as you will have a greater understanding of what foods work for you (and which foods don't). It is possible that you will find that you are no longer choosing any food that is convenient – you'll be thinking before you pop it in your mouth! Following the Low-FODMAP Diet also enables you to have more structure to your dietary planning. It could be that people may lose weight as a consequence of the change in the style of eating, rather than due to the influence of restricting FODMAPs per se. Don't be fooled, though, there are plenty of low-FODMAP foods that are not-so-healthy, and overindulging in these won't aid any weight loss goals you may have.

“*I just cannot accept that there is nothing people can do, unless it has to do with medication. That is why I was happy to see Sue Shepherd's work. I have passed on her research to people who are suffering from IBS and had no clue they could eat all those things on the Low-FODMAP Diet. You know, Sue ought to be very proud of herself. She will always know that she made a difference in people's lives – what an achievement.*”

LOW-FODMAP FRESH PRODUCE SEASON BY SEASON

Supermarkets manage their fruit and vegetables such that many are available all year around, including times when they are out of season. However growing your own, or heading to the local farmer's market can be a way to enjoy fruit and vegetables at their flavoursome, seasonal best!

SEASON	FRUIT	VEGETABLES
SUMMER	Bananas Berries: blueberries, raspberries, strawberries Honeydew melons Passionfruit Pineapple Cantaloupe/rockmelon Valencia oranges	Capsicums Cucumbers Eggplant Green beans Lettuces and other salad greens Parsnip Potato Pumpkin Radish Sprouts Tomatoes Zucchini
AUTUMN	Bananas Cumquats Grapes Kiwifruit Limes Mandarins Passionfruits Valencia orange	Asian greens: bok choy, choy sum Broccoli Cabbage Capsicums Cucumber Eggplant Fennel bulb Ginger Green beans Kale Lettuces and other salad greens Parsnip Potato Pumpkin (except butternut) Spinach Tomatoes Turnip Zucchini

SEASON	FRUIT	VEGETABLES
WINTER	Bananas Kiwifruit Lemons Limes Mandarins Olives Oranges Rhubarb	Broccoli Cabbage Carrots Celeriac Fennel bulb Kale Kohlrabi Parsnips Potatoes Pumpkin (except butternut) Spinach Swede Turnip
SPRING	Berries: blueberries, strawberries Blood oranges Cantaloupes Cumquats Kiwifruit Lemons Mandarins Pineapple	Asian greens: bok choy, choy sum Broccoli Carrots Cucumbers Green beans Kohlrabi Lettuces Potatoes Radish Silverbeet Spinach Watercress Tomatoes Zucchini

DIETARY FIBRE CONTENT OF SOME LOW-FODMAP FOODS

FOODS	SERVING SIZE	DIETARY FIBRE (GRAMS)
Breads and cereals		
Quinoa, boiled	½ cup	2.5
Bread, fruit, gluten-free	1 slice	3
Bread, gluten-free	1 slice	1–2
Bread, gluten-free, multigrain	1 slice	3
Buckwheat kernels, boiled	1 cup	5
Rice, brown, boiled	½ cup	1.8
Cornflakes, gluten-free	1 cup	0
Polenta	½ cup	2.1
Rice bran	2 tablespoons	3
Rice cakes	2	0.8
Rice flour, brown	¼ cup	1.8
Nuts		
Peanut, raw	½ cup	6.5
Peanut butter	1 tablespoon	1
Popcorn, air-popped plain	2 cups	2.4
Pumpkin seeds (pepitas)	1 tablespoon	0.5
Sesame seeds	1 tablespoon	1
Sunflower seeds	1 tablespoon	2

FOODS	SERVING SIZE	DIETARY FIBRE (GRAMS)
Fruit		
Banana	1 medium	3.1
Blueberries	½ cup	1.8
Cantaloupe/rockmelon	1 slice	1
Honeydew melon	1 slice	1
Kiwifruit, small, peeled	1	2.1
Mandarin	1 medium	1.4
Orange	1 medium	3.1
Passionfruit	1 (with seeds)	6
Strawberries	½ cup	1.5
Vegetables		
Capsicum	½ capsicum	1.8
Broccoli, boiled	½ cup	2.6
Carrots, boiled	½ cup	2.4
Green beans, boiled	100 grams	3.2
Mixed vegetables, frozen, boiled	1 cup	4.5
Parsnips, peeled, boiled	½ cup	2.8
Potatoes, unpeeled	1 large	4
Pumpkin (except butternut), peeled	½ cup	1.9
Side salad	1 cup	1.2
Tomato, raw	1 medium	1.8
Zucchini	½ cup	0.7

Sources: Figures adapted from NUTTAB Australia 2006 manufacturers' analyses

HELPFUL RESOURCES

Shepherd Works

This is Dr Sue Shepherd's dietetic consulting practice. Although it's based in Melbourne, Skype consultations are available for people living interstate or overseas. Commencing consultations in 1997, Shepherd Works is Australia's largest gastrointestinal nutrition dietitian practice, and has seen more than 10,000 patients with food intolerances. There are thirteen expert dietitians and two psychologists. Various low-FODMAP and gluten-free cookbooks are available via the website, along with the Low-FODMAP Diet Food Shopping Guide, other relevant resources and a repository of research studies.

www.shepherdworks.com.au

FODMAP Friendly certification logo

This logo appears on food products that have been tested to be low-FODMAP per serve and has been registered around the world. You can eat with confidence the foods that display the logo on their packaging. Visit the website for an up-to-date list of the foods bearing the logo.

www.fodmapfriendly.com

Dietitians Association of Australia

To find an Accredited Practising Dietitian near you, who specialises in gastroenterology and/or food allergies, visit the website.

www.daa.asn.au

Gastroenterological Society of Australia

This is the professional association of Australian gastroenterologists. It has many helpful educational pamphlets for consumers on the website, including a factsheet on the Low-FODMAP Diet.

www.gesa.org.au

IBS Clinic

This IBS psychological support service offers online training to help manage your symptoms.

www.ibsclinic.org.au

THANK YOU

I am thrilled to produce this comprehensive book that can help people navigate their own path to wellness and management of their IBS symptoms. As a dietitian, I see patients with so many dietary needs, it is a great pleasure to produce this book to help you if you need a Low-FODMAP Diet (and you can enjoy the recipes if you are also on a gluten-free diet!)

Thanks to my dear family and my gorgeous fiancé, Adam. I am blessed to have the most wonderful family and partner, you mean the world to me. Thank you also to my most amazing team of dietitians at Shepherd Works. Your work has helped spread the FODMAP message and I am so appreciative of all that you do to make Shepherd Works the home of understanding, professionalism and solutions for patients.

I have enormous gratitude for Ingrid Ohlsson at Pan Macmillan for inviting me to join her on this next FODMAP adventure. You have been inspirational to work with (again!), thank you. Thank you to the other wonderful folk at Pan Macmillan who have helped make this book come to life: Editors Foong Ling Kong, Danielle Walker, Nicola Young; Photographers Jeremy Simons (food shots) and Steven Brown (author shots); Make-Up and Hair Paul Bedggood; Food Stylist Michelle Noerianto; Home Economist John Henseler. Thanks also to Kirby Armstrong for her gorgeous design.

And last, but certainly not least, thank you, the reader, for purchasing this book. I trust you will thoroughly enjoy it from cover to cover.

Best wishes for good health,

Dr Sue Shepherd

INDEX

D

E

F

N

O

P

Q

R

First published 2015 in Macmillan by Pan Macmillan Australia Pty Limited
1 Market Street, Sydney, New South Wales, Australia 2000
This updated edition published in 2017 by Pan Macmillan Australia Pty Limited

A CIP catalogue record for this book is available from the National Library of Australia: http://catalogue.nla.gov.au

Design by Kirby Armstrong
Editing by Foong Ling Kong
Index by Frances Paterson, Olive Grove Indexing Services
Typesetting by Post Pre-press Group
Additional typesetting Kirby Armstrong

Photography by Jeremy Simons
Additional photography by Steven Brown and Rob Palmer
Prop and food styling by Michelle Noerianto
Additional prop and food styling by David Morgan
Food preparation by John Henseler
Additional food preparation by Olivia Andrews

Colour and reproduction by Splitting Image Colour Studio, Clayton, Victoria
Printed and bound by 1010 Printing